Fr. Joe gives us this quick read; reminding us we are all gifted. This means we are all stewards, and expected to be grateful and care for, as well as share, all we are given, including our very lives. His real, lived examples and reflection questions at the end of each chapter help the teaching points gently settle into the soul.

~Julie Kenny, Director of Member Services,
International Catholic Stewardship Council

Enjoyable, educational and reflective read for pastors, parish councils, finance committees, and parish staffs. Grounded in the spirituality of gratitude, hopefulness, and stewardship this book includes real life experiences that can improve our efforts in promoting a call to be a "disciple of our Lord."

~Vito Napoletano, Stewardship Consultant and member of
the USCCB Committee on Stewardship which wrote
the 1992 pastoral letter, Stewardship: A Disciple's Response

This book will be difficult to put down. Readers will find interesting and practical suggestions on developing and implementing membership support in a parish community.

~Marilyn Napoletano, a longtime religious educator
St. Augustine parish in Casselberry, FL.

There is no wonder why Fr. Joe Creedon is such a respected and popular presenter on stewardship. His passion, expertise as a pastor, and understanding of the impact of stewardship as a way of life is unmistakable. I am grateful that now with Stewardship: A Life-Giving Spirituality *people will more widely benefit from his wisdom. You are sure to be inspired to embrace stewardship as a life-giving spirituality. Your life is sure to be enriched as a result.*

~Leisa Anslinger, author, presenter and mentor

Stewardship
A LIFE-GIVING SPIRITUALITY

Rev. Joseph D. Creedon

First Stillwater River Publications Edition

ISBN-13: 978-1-946-30067-6
ISBN-10: 1-946-30067-5

Library of Congress Control Number: 2018950021

1 2 3 4 5 6 7 8 9 10

Written by Rev. Joseph D. Creedon
Cover photo by Jay Swoboda, used with permission.
Cover design by Kody Lavature

Published by Stillwater River Publications, Pawtucket, RI, USA.

Dedication

To my brother, Mike.
He had many gifts; he shared them well!
He was taken from us too soon.

Table of Contents

Foreword i

Acknowledgements iii

Introduction v

Chapter I - Stewardship Is a Spirituality 1

Chapter II - The What and Why of Stewardship 7

Chapter III - Stewardship Begins With a Dream 13

Chapter IV - Receiving God's Gifts Gratefully 19

Chapter V - Developing God's Gifts Responsibly...................25

Chapter VI - Sharing Our Gifts Lovingly With Others 31

Chapter VII - Make A Return With Increase to the Lord 37

Chapter VIII - It Is Baptism That Makes Us
Stewards/Disciples..43

Chapter IX - Confirmation, The Gift That Keeps Giving........51

Chapter X - Eucharist: Let Us Give Thanks to the Lord,
Our God 59

Chapter XI - Reconciliation, the Anointing of the Sick,
Marriage and Holy Orders: Four More Gifts
From God..65

Chapter XII – Stewardship: Time to Start Living
the Dream 77

Foreword

Nine years ago, I first heard the Rev. Joseph Creedon address an audience on the spirituality of Christian stewardship. I knew then that Joe, as he prefers to be called, was indeed one of the most informed and authoritative voices on this ancient Christian concept that I had heard speak.

Catholics have begun to rediscover the Gospel imperative of stewardship, especially in the last 25 years since the publication of the pastoral letter of the United States Catholic bishops, *Stewardship: A Disciple's Response*. But there is still a dearth of good resource materials on the subject and with *Stewardship: A Life-Giving Spirituality*, Joe does his part to fill that void.

Stewardship is a general introduction to the concept of Christian stewardship in the Catholic tradition. Rooted in Joe's decades-long study, prayer, pastoral leadership and teaching, his writing has the force of his in-depth knowledge and experience.

Joe brings to life the spirituality of Christian stewardship and explores its deep yet practical dimensions, mining that place in the soul where faith meets understanding. As a teacher, Joe helps the reader see this ancient biblical concept as if for the first time. He devotes four chapters to unwrapping the bishops' pastoral letter. Throughout, the reader might imagine being a member of his parish when Joe first asked them to "become stewards of the Good News of Jesus Christ."

Joe makes the theology of stewardship accessible. In chapters describing how the Church's sacraments inform our understanding of stewardship in the Catholic tradition, Joe reveals how the sacraments reflect Christ's active, loving presence in the world. As members of the mystical body of Christ, stewardship encourages us to live Christ's mission of love, peace and reconciliation in our own lives.

In addition, Stewardship reveals Joe to be a stylist. He takes a concept, an anecdote or a scripture quote and elaborates on it, using it to support his basic theme. As he writes about the sacrament of matrimony, for example, he describes it as a "most personal sacrament," yet says of the couple, "They are signs of God's love for all people … And our world is in desperate need of signs of God's love." This sacramental character is the essence of the life of a steward.

Joe has the gift of a story-teller and possesses a keen wit. I found myself smiling often. But most importantly, Joe is at his core a man of deep faith. Stewardship reveals a life lived for the Gospel. He cherishes the church's rich history, even though he is not soft with his critiques, and he embodies what is near the heart of the Catholic faith, a welcoming hospitality and "an attitude of gratitude."

When I've had the opportunity to attend a conference, seminar or retreat where Joe has spoken, invariably I hear one or more members of his audience say: "You should have heard Father Creedon!" I often have. And thanks to print media, you can get a glimpse into what his audiences are talking about. Perhaps others will be encouraged by Joe's efforts to add to the growing list of resources on the spirituality of Christian stewardship. Joe will be a hard act to follow—but a blessed one.

Michael Murphy
Executive Director
International Catholic Stewardship Council

Acknowledgements

There are so many folks to be thanked. Where do I begin? I need to thank my parents; they taught me how to say please and thank you. They made sure I appreciated what I had. They encouraged me to develop my gifts; they taught me how to share them. They made faith in God the center of our family. Harry and Kitty Creedon were good stewards without ever knowing the word.

This book would never have been printed if it were not for the stewards of Christ the King Parish where I was the Parish Priest for thirty-one years. They not only allowed me to dream, they actively encouraged it. We journeyed together creating a dynamic stewardship parish. The parish staff bought into the vision of a parish where everyone was expected to be part of the action. Nancy Drennan was my Pastoral Associate for many years. She kept me on task; she challenged or affirmed me when necessary. I don't know a better steward of the gifts God has given her.

Writing a book is not an easy task. Once I thought the book was finished, I learned that it had just begun. I shared the nascent manuscript with friends. Nancy Drennan was first; as always she challenged and affirmed me. Next I shared it with my friend, Sr. Susan Donohue, FCJ, who made more suggestions. Then Phil and Sarah Tracy had a go at it. They offered both substantive and grammatical suggestions. Thinking I was close to the finish line, I sent the manuscript to Sallie Sirhal who has patiently edited many of my written efforts. As always, she was very thorough. I am always both thankful and amazed at how many things she can find wrong with what I think is an almost flawless manuscript.

When my oldest brother, Jerry, was home on vacation, I asked him if he would read my manuscript. He is a believer but not well versed in the concept of stewardship. As always he was very thorough. At the end of his vacation, we sat down and went through the manuscript page by page.

Auxiliary Bishop Robert Morneau of Green Bay, Wisconsin, was kind enough to read my manuscript and make a few suggestions. My good friend and brother priest, Jack Lavin, did the same.

Rev. Robert Randall, my college English professor, offered the most devastating review of all. This process went on for more than three years, so I am sure I have forgotten some folks. I ask their understanding and forgiveness. My American College, University of Louvain classmate, friend, brother priest, and scripture scholar, Rev. Frank Maters of the Archdiocese of Hartford also read the manuscript and made several very helpful suggestions.

Michael Murphy, the executive director of the International Catholic Stewardship Council, who has become a friend, was kind enough to write the Foreword for this book. ICSC has been a wonderful experience in my life. I have served on the Board of Directors; I have been invited to speak at a good number of its Annual Conferences. Most of all, I have met and been taught by some very faith-filled stewards at its gatherings. Vito and Marilyn Napoletano, Leisa Anslinger, Julie Kenney and Cindy Bosh, all friends from ICSC, helped the book grow to completion.

It has been my good fortune to travel the United States, Canada, and Great Britain giving Stewardship workshops, parish missions and keynote addresses. Those experiences are the foundation for this book and I thank all who invited me to share my stewardship story in their faith communities.

I am filled with gratitude for all who have knowingly or unknowingly made *Stewardship: Life-Giving Spirituality* a reality.

LET US GIVE THANKS TO THE LORD, OUR GOD

Introduction

*D*uring my fifty years of priestly ministry, I have had a variety of experiences and met some truly wonderful people. Early on, I taught religion in a Catholic high school, next I was a college campus minister. Finally, I became the pastor of a university parish. In these different settings one thing was constant, the people with whom I ministered had a shared hunger for a deeper relationship with God.

What most people lacked, however, was a spirituality that would allow them to have that deeper relationship. Most people did not think they had or needed a spirituality. Indeed the meaning of the word "spirituality" was itself an obstacle. The definition of spirituality that I use is "the lens through which we encounter and respond to God's presence in our lives." The premise of this book is that stewardship is a spirituality that will enrich the lives of all Christians.

My first experience with stewardship was before the American bishops wrote their 1992 Pastoral Letter, *Stewardship: A Disciple's Response*. Before that pastoral letter, stewardship was for many a code word for money. Stewardship was always about Time, Talent, and Treasure. Nevertheless before the bishops' pastoral letter, the approach was grab their money and their Time and Talent will follow. After their pastoral letter, people were invited to share their Time and Talent and their Treasure would follow. Today there are still people who use stewardship as a code word for money, but fortunately their number is dwindling. Hopefully they will soon be extinct. Growing are the people who believe what the bishops said at the beginning of *Stewardship: A Disciple's Response*, "The Christian vocation is essentially a call to be a disciple of Jesus. Stewardship is part of that. Even more to the point, however, Christians are called to be good stewards of the personal vocations they receive. Each of us must discern, accept, and live out joyfully and generously the commitments, responsibilities, and roles to which God calls him or her."

I embraced the spirituality of stewardship more than twenty-nine years ago. My life has never been the same. Over the years, I have witnessed a profound transformation in people's lives when they embraced the spirituality of stewardship.

This book is a distillation of what I have learned on my stewardship journey. It is my hope that it will help you to begin your stewardship journey or encourage you to enter more deeply into the spirituality called Stewardship.

Rev. Joseph Creedon

Stewardship

A LIFE-GIVING SPIRITUALITY

Chapter I

STEWARDSHIP IS A SPIRITUALITY

Only when we are prepared to acknowledge
that human beings have also an intrinsic spiritual reality
however that may be expressed –
can we do justice to human flourishing.

Society and Vatican II
James Hanvey, *The Tablet*

Stewardship is a scary concept for many. We live in a time when our personal faith/belief systems have been privatized to an extent that is clearly unhealthy. Put more bluntly: We are afraid to speak about what we believe. When it comes to faith, our politically correct conditioning inclines us to adapt the "live and let live" philosophy so that it becomes a "believe and let believe" mantra. We don't talk about our faith and we don't want to listen to others talking about their faith!

In the many years I have served Christ's church as a priest, I have noticed that lay people are frequently afraid to share their spirituality. If I am invited to someone's home to share a meal, I am frequently asked to say grace before meals. I usually decline not because I don't like to pray but because I like to listen to the prayers of others. My not accepting the invitation to say grace usually leads to a few moments of uncomfortable silence. Usually a child will then be

1

invited to pray and will do so without discomfort because she has not yet learned to be self-conscious about who she is or the quality of her prayer. I have watched parents burst with pride as their child recites the familiar, "Bless us, O Lord, and these thy gifts which we are about to receive from your merciful bounty, Amen." And I have watched parents blush with embarrassment when their child says, "Ruba dub dub, thanks for the grub. Yea, God!"

If an adult elects to say grace, a similar thing happens. Most quickly resort to a long ago memorized grace before meals. A few, and I am pleased to note that their number is growing, will bow their heads, reach out, and grasp a hand of those seated next to them, and speak from the heart their gratitude for the events of the day, the gift of the food and the love of those with whom they will share this meal.

I am not so naive that I don't realize that clericalism is afoot when believing folks habitually defer to the ordained priest when it is time for prayer. Even though the Second Vatican Council, in *Lumen Gentium*, clearly stated, "Fortified by so many and such powerful means of salvation, all the faithful, whatever their condition or state, are called by the Lord, each in his own way, to that perfect holiness whereby the Father is perfect" (LG 11). We have miles to go before the whole People of God embrace enthusiastically the universal call to holiness.

Based on observation and countless conversations during my many years of ministry, I have come to the conclusion that many laypeople expect religious men and women to have a spirituality but they don't expect to have one themselves. I firmly believe that the spirituality of stewardship can help correct this false premise.

Let's begin the corrective process by coming up with a definition of spirituality. I believe that the best and most barebones definition of spirituality is: "The lens through which we encounter and respond to God's presence in our lives." This definition works for female or male, ordained or non-ordained, professed religious or non-professed. In other words it works for all the baptized.

It is a given that the baptized members of our church who respond to God's call by joining a religious order will embrace the spirituality based on the charism of their order. Ignatian spirituality, the spirituality of the Jesuits, is based on the phrase "*Ad majorem Dei Gloriam*"—All for the greater glory of God. Countless graduates of Jesuit places of learning have been taught to write AMDG on the top of all their papers. Many laypeople have embraced this spirituality and have made Ignatian retreats with wonderful results. Nevertheless, Ignatian spirituality was designed for those professed Jesuits who live in community. For those not living in such a community, Ignatian spirituality is at best a hybrid. The same is true for the major religious orders. Franciscan spirituality is based on the preferential option for the poor. Dominican spirituality is based on their mottos; first is *Veritas*—Truth, second is *Laudare, Benedicare, Praedicare*—to praise, to bless, and to preach, the third is *Contemplare et Contemplata Aliis Tradere*—to contemplate and to give to others the fruit of contemplation. Benedictine spirituality likewise flows from their motto: *Ora Et Labore*—to pray and to work. Obviously the Roman Catholic Church has been and is wonderfully enriched by these and other spiritualities but that is not the point. The point is that the overwhelming number of Catholics do not live in a religious community.

When I was in seminary, we were given a monastic or religious spirituality. We lived in community and our days were regulated by the ringing of the bell, which was referred to as "the voice of God." This form of spirituality worked very well when I was in the seminary. But I was called to be a diocesan priest not a monk or a religious. From the day I was ordained the only bells I have heard are the doorbell and the ringing of the phone, both of which brought interruption rather than order to my life. I quickly learned that the spirituality given to me during formation would not work in my life as a diocesan priest. I had to find a new spirituality.

My search for a new spirituality finally brought me to stewardship. My interest in stewardship was first piqued because I was looking for ways to get members of the parish more involved in the life of the parish. It was while I was searching for ways to present the spirituality of stewardship to members of the parish that it dawned on me that if I were going to ask others to do something, I had to be willing to do it myself—always a good philosophy. My journey from introducing stewardship to embracing it for myself was an axial moment in my life as both a believer and as a priest.

I embraced stewardship before the American Bishops wrote their wonderful 1992 Pastoral Letter, *Stewardship: A Disciple's Response*. That document gave me a vocabulary to better explain stewardship and a format to help me evaluate my efforts to both embrace and live stewardship. The bishops provided this assistance with their four-step explanation of what it means to be a good steward or an authentic disciple of Jesus Christ.

When the parish leadership team first introduced stewardship and when I first embraced it, we asked members of the parish to become stewards of the Good News of Jesus Christ. In the parish bulletin, we did not ask for volunteers; we asked for stewards. Nevertheless both then and now the word "steward" has a feeling of uncomfortableness that clings to it. It is a word that has fallen out of use in our everyday lives. The only time we refer to someone as a steward is if we happen to find ourselves on a cruise ship and we need something. The American bishops offered a partial solution to this antiquated vocabulary problem when, in the subtitle of their Pastoral Letter, they used the word "disciple." I say a partial solution because they use "disciple" in the subtitle but use "steward" and "disciple" interchangeably in the text. The search for the right word is ongoing; the solution is fluid. My advice is to use whatever word speaks most clearly to your heart and the living out of your baptismal commitment.

The bishops explained stewardship as a four-step process: "What identifies a steward? Safeguarding material and human resources and using them responsibly are one answer; so is generously giving of time, talent and treasure. But being a Christian steward means more. As Christian stewards, (1) we receive God's gifts gratefully, (2) cultivate them responsibly, (3) share them lovingly in justice with others, and (4) return them with increase to the Lord." (the numbers are not part of the original text). These four attributes will be the subject for chapters IV - VII.

STUDY QUESTIONS:

1. Can you articulate your personal spirituality?

2. What makes speaking about your faith or spirituality a challenge?

3. According to the American Bishops' Pastoral Letter, *Steward-ship: A Disciple's Response*, what are the 4 characteristics of a good steward?

Chapter II

THE WHAT AND WHY
OF STEWARDSHIP

The Christian vocation is essentially a call to be
a disciple of Jesus. Stewardship is part of that.
Even more to the point, however, Christians are called
to be good stewards of the personal vocations they receive.
Each of us must discern, accept, and live out joyfully and generously the
commitments, responsibilities, and roles to which God calls him or her.

National Conference of Catholic Bishops
Stewardship: A Disciple's Response

The biblical notion of stewardship is rooted in a concept that is difficult for us inhabitants of the 21st century to accept— God is the owner of everything! In Genesis 2:15, we are given the roots of stewardship, "The Lord God then took the man and settled him in the Garden of Eden, to cultivate and care for it." God made the earth; God made Adam and Eve. Then he loaned the world to them so that they could care for it. Adam and Eve are the first stewards of creation. Their eating of the forbidden fruit has many meanings but one meaning is certainly that they tried to make themselves gods. They wanted to "own" what was "loaned" to them as gift for safekeeping. We have been repeating their sin ever since.

The biblical concept of a jubilee year (every fifty years) as explained in Leviticus 25 makes it clear that everything belongs to God and is merely loaned to us as tenants, trustees, or stewards. Debts were forgiven and land was returned to its original owner to serve as a reminder that God, not we, owns the land. The Old Testament concept of the tithe was likewise a reminder that God owns everything and it is merely loaned to us.

The concept of stewardship continued to evolve in the New Testament as is evident in the three gospel parables concerning good and bad stewards. (The New American Bible uses the word "manager," whereas the Jerusalem Bible uses the word "steward," for that reason I will be quoting from the Jerusalem Bible.) In Luke 16:1-8, we have the familiar story of the "crafty steward." A few lines from that Gospel should refresh your memory. "There was a rich man and he had a steward who was denounced to him for being wasteful with his property. He called for the man and said, 'What is this I hear about you? Draw up an account of your stewardship because you are not to be my steward any longer'." From there the parable tells how that steward decides to feather his nest so that folks would take care of him when he is fired. He is called clever and crafty but we should never forget that his problems began because he failed to remember that he was entrusted with the master's property. Both before and after he was caught his sin was the same—he allowed himself to be deluded into thinking and acting as if the master's property were his own. He forgot that he was to manage what the master had entrusted to him.

Earlier in Luke (Lk 12:35-48) we have another example of stewardship and accountability. This time Luke uses the image of servants waiting for their master to return from a wedding and the need to always be ready for that return. As this parable continues, Peter asks for a clarification and Jesus continues his teaching on stewardship with this question, "What sort of steward, then, is faithful and wise enough for the master to place him over his household and to give them their allowance of food at the proper time?"

This lesson on being held accountable for our stewardship of all God's gifts ends with a very sobering line, "When a man has had a great deal given to him, a great deal will be demanded of him; when a man has had a great deal given him on trust, even more will be expected of him." For our final Gospel parable we will go to Matthew 25. It is the parable of the three servants (stewards). One is given five talents, one is given two talents, and the last servant is given one talent. The one with five talents makes five more, the one with two gains two more, but the one who is given one talent does nothing with what was given to him. The two servants who use their talents wisely are praised by the master; the one who is fearful of the gift he has been given is stripped of what he was given. I have always wished there was a fourth servant who tried to use what he was given as gift and failed because if there were a fourth servant I am sure that the master would have said to him, "Here are three more, try again." This parable is not about success but about remembering our need to give thanks to God for the gifts he has placed in our lives.

This parable comes right before Matthew's beautiful and chilling account of the Last Judgment where we are reminded that when our life is over God will judge us on how we shared our gifts with others. The time will come when we get to ask, as did the folks in Matthew (Matt 25:31-46), "Lord, when did we see you hungry or thirsty, a stranger or naked, sick or in prison, and did not come to your help?" Then he will answer, "I tell you solemnly, in so far as you neglected to do this to the least of these, you neglected to do it to me. And they will go away to eternal punishment and the virtuous to eternal life." The evolved notion of stewardship in the New Testament does not end with the four Gospels. Paul, in his First Letter to the

Corinthians, offers powerful witness to his vision of stewardship, "People must think of us as Christ's servants, stewards entrusted with the mysteries of God. What is expected of stewards is that each one should be found worthy of his trust." (1 Cor. 4:1-2) Paul sees all believers as "stewards entrusted with the mysteries of God." I don't know about you but I find that job description for believers to be both awe inspiring and frightening. It is a concept that will require much meditation and even more commitment on our part.

Peter in his First Letter continues the notion of stewardship, "Each one of you has received a special grace, so, like good stewards responsible for all these different graces of God, put yourselves at the service of others. If you are a speaker, speak in words which seem to come from God, if you are a helper, help as though every action was done at God's orders; so that in everything God may receive the glory, through Jesus Christ, since to him alone belong all glory and power for ever and ever. Amen." (1 Peter 4:9-11) I hope you are beginning to understand the challenge of stewardship.

God has given each and every one of us the gift of faith in Baptism. At Baptism, we are given both a mission and a ministry. The mission: to become disciples of Jesus and stewards of God's gifts; the ministry is to use our unique gifts and talents in a way that gives glory to God. We will consider this more fully in Chapter VIII.

Stewardship then is a spirituality rooted in the Bible and based on the principle that, "everything we have is a gift from God." Why is the biblically rooted spirituality of stewardship important? Because as our mothers taught us at a very early age and continued to teach us as long as they lived, when someone gives you a gift you should say "Thank You!" They likewise made it abundantly clear that "Thank You" had to be more than words; "Thank You" had to lead to action.

STUDY QUESTIONS:

1. Why is it important to realize that Stewardship is rooted in both the Old and the New Testament?

2. What does it mean to you that you are entrusted with the mysteries of God?

3. Can you identify God's special grace to you?

Chapter III

STEWARDSHIP BEGINS WITH A DREAM

"Which possibility bears the greater pain –
to have died believing in a dream that failed
or to have lived and never known?"

Joseph Juknialis
Winter Dreams

J had a dream last night. It was a variation of a recurring dream that I have been having for years. In the more standard version of the dream, members of the parish are on a bicycle trip. I spend the whole dream in a van going to the end of the line picking up the stragglers and transporting them to the front of the line. I have always consoled myself by saying that the dream has biblical roots in the "first shall be last and the last shall be first" tradition but I fear that others will see something less healthy as the source of my recurring dream.

Why have I chosen to share this dream with people I have never met? I hope that no one will feel obliged to analyze my dream or to share their professional or amateur conclusions with me. I am already way behind on dealing with the problems I know I have without well-intended folks adding to the list. I share this dream because dreams are one of God's preferred methods of

13

communication. In our dreams, imagination trumps reality; we are freed to think outside the box. A quick review of the Bible will show how often God uses sleep, dreams, and trances to break through our defenses.

In the very first book of the Bible (Gen 2:21), we are told that God put Adam into a deep sleep and then took out a rib and made for him a suitable partner, Eve. There is a humorous take on this event that I heard many years ago. It seems that the devil was there at the beginning of creation and watched God create Adam and Eve. When Adam saw Eve, he said, "Man and woman what a great idea." When Eve saw Adam, she said, "Woman and man what a great idea." And the devil smiled because problems had already begun. However you look at it, it all began with a deep sleep.

Elsewhere in Genesis, Joseph has his dreams of the dancing sheaves of wheat and of the sun, the moon, and the stars bowing down to him. (Gen 37:5-11) Joseph shares his dreams with his brothers and trouble begins when he goes to meet up with his brothers in Shechem. When they see him coming to them do you remember what they said? "Here comes that master dreamer! Let us kill him and throw him into one of the cisterns here; we could say that a wild beast devoured him. We shall then see what comes of his dreams." (Gen 37:19-20)

In I Kings 3:4-15, we are told that the Lord appeared to Solomon in a dream and God said to him, "Ask something of me and I will give it to you," and Solomon answered, "Give your servant, therefore, an understanding heart to judge your people and distinguish right from wrong. For who is able to govern this vast people of yours?" Solomon went on to be praised for his wisdom but sometimes we forget that it all began with a dream.

The prophet Jonah made his way through the great city of Nineveh preaching repentance. To his surprise and dismay his message was heard and following the leadership of the King everyone repented and the Lord "repented of the evil that he had threatened to do to them." When Jonah grew angry at God's forgiveness he wanted to die. (Jonah Ch. 4) He only came to understand God's mercy when "he grew faint" under the withering heat once God killed the gourd plant that had provided him shade. "Grew faint" is just another way of identifying how God speaks to us when our rational side is suspended.

The dream-communications do not end with the Old Testament. Matthew recounts: "Now this is how the birth of Jesus came about. When his mother Mary was engaged to Joseph, but before they lived together, she was found with child through the power of the Holy Spirit. Joseph her husband, an upright man unwilling to expose her to the law, decided to divorce her quietly. Such was his intention when suddenly the angel of the Lord appeared in a dream and said to him: Joseph, Son of David, have no fear about taking Mary as your wife." (Mt. 1:18-30) And this was not the end of Joseph's dreams. The angel appeared to him again in a dream and he fled to Egypt with Jesus and Mary. Just before Joseph had his second dream, the Wise Men had a dream so they did not go back to Herod and they returned home by another route. (Matt 2:12-14)

Likewise one of the first challenges in the early Church was resolved by a dream. The whole issue of the Gentiles as members of the early Church was solved by a series of dreams. First Cornelius, the Roman centurion, had his vision, then Peter fell into a "trance" on the rooftop and had his vision of the sheet being lowered down with both clean and unclean animals. The Lord told him to slaughter and eat the animals but Peter balked saying, "Sir, it is unthinkable! I have never eaten anything unclean or impure in my life." God trumps his protestations by saying, "What God has purified you are not to call unclean." (Acts 10:1-16)

The above accounting of dream/vision stories certainly does not exhaust the dream/vision stories in the Bible but are offered as examples of how God speaks to his people and his people sometimes listen better when their logical objections are suspended. The Bible is full of dreamers and the Master Dreamer (the Divine Dreamer) is Jesus himself as Joseph Juknialis points out beautifully in his book, *Rest Stops for The Soul.*

To embrace Stewardship one has to be a dreamer. The American Bishops were dreamers when, in 1992, they wrote, *Stewardship: A Disciple's Response.* They were not writing about what was but what could be. Anyone who chooses to live the spirituality of stewardship must be a dreamer; must be open to what can be rather than what is or has been. I introduced the spirituality of stewardship to my parish more than 25 years ago. Before I asked the parish to embrace stewardship, I personally embraced the spirituality of stewardship as my way of life. From that day forward my life and ministry have never been the same. I hope and pray that the same will be true for you!

Anthony DeMello in his book, *Song of The Bird,* shares this wonderful thought in a mini-parable called *Music To The Deaf,* "I used to be stone deaf. I would see people stand up and go through all kinds of gyrations. They called it dancing. It looked absurd to me—until one day I heard the music." The music of stewardship has been playing in our hearts since the day of our Baptism. The problem is that too often we have been deaf to it. Hopefully I can help you hear that music.

As St. Paul says in 1 Corinthians 13:12, "Now we see indistinctly, as in a mirror; then we shall see face to face." I am convinced that the spirituality of stewardship is an excellent guide as we journey from where we are to where God is calling us to be.

STUDY QUESTIONS:

1. Where do you think you are deaf to the call of God?

2. Do you believe that God has a plan for your life? How would your life change if you fully committed to being a good steward of all God's gifts?

Chapter IV

RECEIVING GOD'S GIFTS GRATEFULLY

To be grateful for the good things
that happen in our lives is easy,
but to be grateful for all of our lives
– the good as well as the bad,
the moments of joy as well as the moments of sorrow,
the successes as well as the failures,
the rewards as well as the rejections
– that requires hard spiritual work.

Henri Nouwen
Bread for the Journey

Our mothers taught us, at an early age, to say "Thank You" whenever we received a gift. At about the same time, they also taught us two other very important life-virtues—always to say "please" when we ask for something and always to share whatever gifts we receive. We were taught these foundational virtues— please, thank you, and sharing—at a very early age. These foundational virtues are basic stewardship values. They were not taught to us as part of the spirituality of stewardship but they were taught to us, which leads to an important discovery. The core values of stewardship have been part of our lives from the very beginning. The word

19

"stewardship" may be new to our vocabulary but its synergy has always been there.

If we are to embrace fully the spirituality of stewardship, we must embrace the reality that "everything we have is a gift from God." We must develop "the attitude of gratitude." I wish I knew who first coined that phrase. It is usually attributed to Archbishop Thomas Murphy, the father of stewardship for the Catholic Church in America, but he may just have been the one who made it popular. In the end, the messenger is not as important as the message.

It is not easy to embrace the fact that "everything we have is a gift from God." Most of us, at a subliminal level, believe that everything we have is a result of our own efforts. The following story points out how persistent this false conclusion can be. The setting for the story is the Irish countryside; the focus is an abandoned farmhouse. A stranger buys the dilapidated farmhouse and immediately begins to make improvements. The stonewalls are rebuilt, the house gets a new coat of whitewash, the fields are plowed and planted and the thatched roof is repaired. The people in the nearby village watch all this work with curiosity and wonder. One thing they know for certain is that whoever the new owner is he never goes to church. A group of the villagers go to the parish priest and convince him to meet the new owner and to invite him to church. Soon thereafter the parish priest goes out to the newly restored farmhouse and knocks on the door. The door is opened; the priest is greeted and soon finds himself seated at the kitchen table enjoying a cup of tea and homemade scones. After the proscribed small talk, the priest zeroes in on the purpose of his visit. He says to the new owner, "I love what you and God have done with this place." The new owner pauses, takes a sip of tea and says, "Father do you remember what the place looked like when God had it all to Himself?"

The story is both humorous and tragic. Humorous because it invites us to laugh at ourselves. Tragic because it lays bare the fact that we are inclined to take too much credit for our successes and too little blame for our failures. The new owner's heart is not filled with gratitude because his heart is too full of pride in his own accomplishments. Needless to say, he is not alone in this attitude.

The best antidote I have discovered for the hubris of our sense of self-importance is to set aside time to compile a list of the gifts we have received from God.

THE GIFT OF LIFE: Life is a gift from God. None of us did anything to deserve being born. Just spend a few moments getting in touch with the odds of being born. Spend a few moments being thankful for still being alive. The longer I live the more I realize that life is a gift. My younger brother, Mike, died at the age of 56, way too soon. He was a delightful human being, a loving husband, father, teacher, coach, and friend. He died too young. His family and my brothers and I could focus on what was taken from us or focus on the gift of having him in our lives for whatever part of his 56 years we shared. Life is a gift and we need to live each day thanking God for it.

THE GIFT OF FAMILY: Just as we did nothing to deserve being born, we did nothing to deserve the parents and siblings we were given. Sometimes it takes time to fully appreciate the gift of family. There were times when I would have traded in my parents for another set that would have met my perceived needs of the moment. Fortunately, I have lived long enough to realize that they were the best parents for me. My older brother, Jerry, has expressed it this way, "Our father demanded perfection and our mother convinced us that we could live up to his expectation." Once we embrace family as gift, it is amazing how the things that could drive us apart lose their power.

THE GIFT OF EDUCATION: I have never met anyone who did not have a story about a teacher who changed her/his life. I have my list of such teachers; I'm sure you have yours. Education has changed our worldview and our self-understanding. Most of our education takes place in a classroom setting but some does not. We have learned from coaches, scout leaders, neighbors, relatives, and friends. All learning is a gift from God. We need to be more thankful for the gift of our education.

THE GIFT OF VOCATION: Nothing in life is as important as discovering what God wants us to do with our lives. I truly believe that God wanted me to be a priest. I could give you many reasons why I should have found another vocation but in the end God won out. Many people seem to get lost in their search to discover who and what God wants them to be but the happiest and most fulfilled people I know are those who are doing what they love and love what they are doing. Is there a better gift than that?

THE GIFT OF FRIENDS: Let us say together, "We do not deserve the friends we have!" The gift of friendship is so precious. Our friends love us not in spite of our faults but because of them. Our friends see our potential better than we do. Friends encourage us to grow and take risks. Friends teach us that time is a gift when they choose to share time with us. Most important of all, our friends see our gifts and talents before we do and they lovingly encourage us to recognize and develop our hidden gifts.

The above list of gifts is not meant to be exhaustive; it is offered as an outline. I hope you will use it to create your own list of gifts. Unless we make ourselves aware of the many gifts God has sown in our lives we will never develop the "attitude of gratitude" that is essential for the spirituality of stewardship to take root in our lives.

STUDY QUESTIONS:

1. How can you deepen your appreciation of the importance of saying, "please" and "thank you" along with the importance of sharing the gifts we receive?

2. What will help us realize more fully that everything we have is a gift from God?

3. What is the most precious gift God has given you? Why is it most precious?

Chapter V

DEVELOPING GOD'S GIFTS RESPONSIBLY

After the beggar died someone took the bowl
that he used for begging and cleaned it up.
Much to his surprise he discovered that the beggar's bowl
was made of pure gold.
The beggar never knew he had no need to beg.

From this storyteller's memory
Without benefit of original source

did not know whether I should have ended the last chapter or begun this chapter with a discussion of the gifts we have that we don't know we have. In the end, I concluded that its placement was not as important as the message. In so many ways, we are like the beggar mentioned at the beginning of this chapter; we don't realize the gifts we possess! Before we can develop a gift we have to know we have it. Once we know we have a gift, we have to believe in the gift and commit ourselves to developing it.

Lists of famous failures appear, now and again, in newspapers or magazines. These lists have always fascinated me. I'm sure you know some of them. Albert Einstein did not speak until he was four and did not read until he was seven. A news editor fired Walt Disney because "he lacked imagination." Michael Jordan and Bob

Cousy were both cut from their high school basketball teams. Bill Gates dropped out of Harvard and his first business venture failed. Winston Churchill failed the sixth grade and was defeated in every election until he was elected Prime Minister of England at the age of 62. Stephen King was so frustrated with his first novel, *Carrie*, that he threw it away. His wife found it in the trash and took it out. This list could obviously be longer but in the back of my head I can hear my father's voice saying, "Once you've made your point, don't beat it to death!"

God has blessed us with many gifts. Some we realize early on in our lives; others lie undiscovered and dormant. One of life's greatest challenges is to discover and develop all of our God-given gifts. Parents, siblings, teachers, coaches, scout leaders, and friends play an important role in our gift-discovery journey.

I have always been fascinated by what I call refrigerator art. Whenever I visit someone's home, I am always on the lookout for children's artwork on the refrigerator door. When I was a pastor, children would frequently come out of church and hand me a drawing and say, "I made this for you." Sometimes the artwork would be on a page ripped out of a hymnal or part of the Sunday bulletin. I learned to overlook that so I could focus on the gift. I would always say, "Thank You" and I would, if possible, put the drawing on my refrigerator door not for its artistic value but for its symbolic value. Some of the children's drawings showed real promise; others not so much. All of them represented a deep desire to make a connection, to begin a relationship and that is the greatest gift of all. We need the encouragement of others; we need to trust them when they see gifts in us that we do not yet see clearly ourselves.

Allow me to share a personal experience that demonstrates this point. Early on in my priestly ministry I was a college campus minister, a ministry that I truly enjoyed. After a few years on campus a member of the administration came to me and asked if I would consider rewriting the student handbook. The request was both flattering and confusing. I had never thought of myself as a writer; I thought of myself as a speaker. My first response to the request was "Why me?" The response was, "Because you understand the students." I asked for a few days to consider the request. Then I went to a friend who taught in the English department and asked her opinion. If she hesitated, it was imperceptible. She told me not to do it because my writing was like a recipe for cocoa. I was not sure what she meant by that but I knew it was not a compliment. I went back to my office, called the administrator and told her that I was flattered but I just had too much on my plate to take on something else.

Many years later, when I was in parish ministry, I was having dinner one evening with the parish director of music and his wife. During the meal his wife, who worked for a Catholic publishing company, asked if I had ever thought of writing a daily Lenten meditation booklet. My mind quickly reminded me of my ability to write recipes for cocoa and I said, "No." She went on to explain that one of the authors they had lined up to write next year's booklet had backed out on them and they needed to find someone new. Once again, I declined but she persisted. Finally she got me to agree to give it a try. I went home and wrote reflections for Ash Wednesday through to the Second Sunday of Lent. I emailed her my efforts certain that she would see that she had been mistaken as to my writing abilities. Two days later, she emailed me and to my surprise said, "Keep going." Her encouragement led to seven Lenten meditation booklets and seven Advent meditation booklets that sold quite well and went who knows where. One thing is certain, without her vision and the encouragement of many people who enjoyed those booklets I would never have written those fourteen booklets and I certainly would not be writing this book.

If you have gotten this far in the book, either you like cocoa or we are connecting through the written word. If you have started the list of personal gifts, as suggested at the end of the last chapter, I invite you, in the not too distant future, to find that list. Next to each gift listed write the name of the person or persons who helped you discover that gift. If you want to go all the way, ask a few of your friends to make a list of what they see as your gifts and then compare your list to theirs. Doing this will be very helpful in developing the "attitude of gratitude" and developing your God given gifts.

Everyone is gifted. Some of our gifts we discover ourselves; other gifts have to be pointed out by others. No matter how we discover our gifts they have to be developed. We have to work on our gifts; we must have the discipline to hone them to perfection. Blessed John Cardinal Newman once said, "Nothing would be done at all if one waited until one could do it so well that no one could find fault with it." Many people are afraid to test out their gifts. Fear of failure, it seems, is pervasive. We are not born with a fear of failure. We develop it as we live. Fear wears many disguises—fear of failure, fear of success, fear of ridicule, fear of not belonging, fear of looking foolish—to name but a few of fear's disguises. All of fear's disguises lead to stagnant energy. Fear always brings with it inertia and inertia always leads to stagnation. No one achieves greatness without risk taking and hard work.

Today my family and friends consider me to be a good cook but that was not always the case. Early on in my culinary pursuits there were more disasters than successes. I remember talking with my mother about learning how to cook. She gave me some great advice. She said, "If you want to be a good cook make sure you eat all your failures." Some of my failures were truly inedible but in general I followed her advice.

Allow me one final example of how we have to work hard to develop our gifts. The example is fairly universal. Do you remember what it was like to learn how to ride a bicycle? We start off with a tricycle and for a while that is enough but soon we want more. We want a bicycle. Finally the day comes when we get our first bicycle but our joy quickly fades when we realize that the bicycle comes with training wheels. So instead of going from three wheels to two wheels we go backwards to four wheels. Finally the fateful day comes when the training wheels are taken off. A person we thought loved us, usually a mother or a father, puts us on the bicycle, puts one hand on the back of the seat and the other on the handlebar, tells us we can do it and pushes us off to fend for ourselves. The result is always the same—we fall to the ground. Then the person we thought loved us picks us up and repeats the process. Eventually we get the hang of it but not before we have fallen and picked ourselves up more often than we choose to remember.

The gift of balance is key to being able to ride a bicycle; the process of discovering that gift is repeated many times in our lives. Life is a series of failures that morph into successes sometimes without our realizing it or knowing how it happens but it does. We had to learn how to be brothers and sisters, we had to learn how to be husbands and wives, and we had to learn how to be friends and neighbors. We need to learn how to be good stewards!

Ed Hayes, the spiritual writer and founder of Shantivanam House of Prayer in Easton, Kansas, was fond of saying, "If something is worth doing, it is worth doing poorly." When I first heard him say it, it led to a long and a not very pleasant conversation. I was offended by his philosophy. I, like many of us, had been hard-wired to believe that if something is worth doing, it is worth doing well. He finally helped me see the wisdom in his point of view. The challenge is not to set a goal of doing things poorly but of being willing to do something poorly with the goal of learning how to do it well.

God has blessed us with many gifts but what good are those gifts if we do not acknowledge, cherish, and develop them?

STUDY QUESTIONS:

1. What is the latest gift you discovered in your life or someone pointed out to you?

2. Are you brave enough to name the fear or fears that keep you from growing?

3. Can you remember a failure that helped you to grow?

Chapter VI

SHARING OUR GIFTS LOVINGLY WITH OTHERS

What we do for ourselves dies with us.
What we do for others and the world remains and is immortal.

Albert Pine

Learning the art of sharing is a gift and a discipline that has to be developed. We learn how to share first and best from our parents. Share with your brother, share with your sister gets repeated over and over again in our formative years until finally we catch on and no longer have to be told.

Many years ago, I was blessed to share in this experience. A mother was teaching her boys to share. She was a young mother dying of cancer. It was Holy Week and I was visiting her in the hospital. Her days were quickly running out. Her family was with her when I came to visit. Someone had given one of the boys a box of Milk Duds; his brothers wanted some of the candy. The boys knew their mother was sick but were too young to know she was dying. Their skirmish was completely incongruous with the unspoken sadness that filled the room. The young mother, even in her dying, was not going to pass up what was to be one of her last acts of parenting. While her husband and I watched she called the boys

31

to her hospital bed. The boys climbed up on the bed. She asked for the box of candy; it was surrendered. She patiently counted out the pieces into three piles. She gave each boy his share of the candy. There was one candy left. She looked at her husband and me, said, "Sorry" and plunked the one surviving piece into her mouth. Words fail to capture the power of her selfless teaching or its example. I know that as I was driving home from that visit, it dawned on me that I had just seen Eucharist celebrated with candy. He took the bread, blessed it, and shared it with them saying, "This is my body which will be given up for you." The power of sharing was etched on my heart that day.

Many ingredients of the spirituality of stewardship are counterintuitive. None more so than this: "Stewardship is based in the need of the giver to give more than on the need of the receiver to receive." Most of us have been conditioned to be need-based givers. If someone has a need they should present their case and, if we agree with both the cause and the need, then we think about giving. Need-based giving is unfortunately the bedrock of most, if not all, church related giving of Time, Talent, and Treasure. It takes a while to unlearn our conditioning to be need-based givers.

Perhaps a personal story will help make my point. Quite a few years ago I was invited to be a partner in a small condominium project. The project was sound and it would result in my being able to buy a condo for a very reasonable price at the end of the project. There was only one small problem. I did not have the money to get in at the ground level. I suppose I could have gone to a bank for a loan but I could not get by the words of President Harry S. Truman, "One thing I don't like about banks is that once you prove to them you don't really need the money they are more than happy to loan it to you." So I called my parents and said I wanted to ask a favor. On the appointed Sunday, I showed up at my parents' home with blueprints and a well-rehearsed presentation. I went on for about a half hour then I sat back and said, "What do you think?" My father thought for a few moments and said, "I think you just wasted a half hour of our time." My heart sank and I began to roll up the blueprints. As I slipped the elastic band around the blueprints my father said, "Of course we will loan you the money. Why did you think you had to sell us on the idea?" My parents' need to share with me was much greater than their need to approve of the project. Don't get me wrong, they needed some reassurance that my project was sound but not as much as I felt I had to give them. They loaned me the money. I bought a condo; I paid them back in full. Many times since that day, I have been able to "pay it forward" as they say. Frequently when I am in a position to help someone out with Time, Talent, or Treasure I do so with a joyful heart because of my parents, because of my faith, because of the stewardship planted in my heart. When the recipients of my sharing say, "Thank You" I always tell them don't thank me thank my parents.

In Acts 20:33-34 we are told, "I did this to show you that this is how we must exert ourselves to support the weak, remembering the words of the Lord Jesus, who himself said, 'there is more happiness in giving than receiving'." This quote is important for two reasons. First, nowhere in the Gospel is Jesus reported to have said it; secondly it is a quote that must be carefully nuanced. While it is true that it is "better to give than receive," this truism needs to be balanced. Henri Nouwen, one of my favorite spiritual authors, said, "If I can only give and not receive, then the only honest thing to do is question why I give." A good priest-friend of mine, who has now gone home to be with God, used to love to entertain. Once grace had been said and his guests had been seated he would stand at his place, raise a glass of wine and say, "To my guests, may they soon be my hosts!" He did this because he had discovered that there has to be a balance between giving and receiving. To give is to be in control; to receive is to be vulnerable. How many times have you learned from a friend that she needed help but did not ask for it? How many times have you been offended because that friend did not ask for help? How many times have you needed help but did not ask for it?

True sharing can happen only if it is reciprocal. If we enjoy giving then we should be willing to receive as well. Only a small percentage of us will ever be able to enjoy receiving but that should be our goal. Many of us are experts at what is called prayer of petition. That is when we pray asking for something but even here we need to grow. Whenever I visit folks in the hospital there is always a time for prayer. When the patient is terminal, I always ask if there were anything she would like to ask for in prayer. The responses I get are most often a surprise. The patient wants to pray for her family, her parents, the doctors and nurses. Seldom does the sick person want to pray for herself. Even in the face of death many of us find it difficult to ask for divine assistance.

It is good to give a friend a listening ear; it is better if there are times when we are the speaker and allow our friend to be the listener. It is good when we carve spaces in our schedules to be present to a neighbor; it is better if there are times when we are willing to ask our neighbor to carve out time for us. One of the mysteries of our Christian faith is that it is not based on either/or but both/and. With our faith it is not virgin or mother but virgin and mother. It is not human or divine but human and divine. With our faith it is not saint or sinner but sinner and saint. It is not in the world or out of the world but in the world but not of the world. It is not giving or receiving but giving and receiving.

What good is done if we are willing to give to others but are not willing to receive from them as well?

STUDY QUESTIONS

1. What is the most powerful act of sharing that you can remember?

2. Who is the best sharer you know? Why is she/he such a good sharer?

3. Why is it so difficult for you to ask for help?

Chapter VII

MAKE A RETURN WITH INCREASE TO THE LORD

Imagine at death, coming before the Lord.
He welcomes me and then says, "How well
did you use the abilities, time and material goods
that I gave you to make the world a better place?"

The Little Burgundy Book
Diocese of Saginaw

The rock-solid foundation of all stewardship is believing and acting on the fact "that everything we have is a gift from God." The challenge is, of course, that it is always easier to say it than to live it! Stewardship is not easy to live but living our lives with a steward's heart will fill our hearts with joy that will overflow into the lives of all we meet.

The fourth and final stage of stewardship—making a return with increase to the Lord—sounds like a form of spiritual accounting but that is not the case. In most cases, the increase is more ethereal than material.

Back in Chapter II when I was laying out the scriptural basis for Stewardship I referenced the parable of the three servants. Hopefully you remember the parable. The master gives one servant five talents, another two talents, and finally one servant gets one talent. Two use their talents wisely and make a return to the Master with an increase. The one-talent servant did nothing with his gift but merely returned it to the Master. As I said in Chapter II this parable is not about success but about risk taking. It is about using the gifts that God has given us. It is important to realize that this parable immediately precedes Matthew's chilling account of the final judgment. The entire world is separated into two groups—the sheep and the goats. The sheep are placed at the right and the goats are placed on the left of the Son of Man. Those on the right are rewarded; those on the left are punished. The measuring rod is how they treated those in need—the hungry, the stranger, the sick, the naked, and those in prison. Both the saved and the punished ask, "When did we see you hungry or thirsty, a stranger or naked, sick or in prison and did not come to help you?" And the Son of Man answered them, "I tell you solemnly, in so far as you neglected to do it to one of the least of these, you neglected to do it to me."

What is important in this account of the final judgment is the Son of Man reminds us that the way we make a return to God includes the way we treat others. This insight is helpful as we attempt to plumb the depth of meaning in the fourth and final step of being a good steward: "To make a return with increase to the Lord."

God gives us the gifts of Time, Talent, and Treasure and he awaits our return on these gifts. Some of the return will be focused on God. We need to find the time to pray, to find the time to dialogue with God. Without prayer we are certain to lose our way; to get lost in the pursuit of things that don't really matter. When we find the time to pray, we make a return with increase to the Lord.

We are called to use our talents to worship God. Every Sunday, in every parish throughout the world, the gathered community is enriched by the sharing of talents that is our worship. Some have the gift of greeting those who come to worship, others have the gift of music or song, and still others have the gift of proclaiming God's word. All have the gift of listening and responding with full voice. When we worship God in the Eucharistic community, we make a return with increase to the Lord. Whereas all are given the same gift of Time, the gift of today, not all are given the same Talents. Likewise not all are given the same Treasure but all are given Treasure. We are called to make a Treasure return to the Lord with increase when we gather to worship and the basket is passed. I remember reading somewhere that when the basket is passed there are three kinds of givers— the obligation givers, the grudge givers and the thanks-givers. In other words, when the basket is passed some give because they ought to, some give because they have to, and some give because they want to. As stewards, we are called to be thanks-givers.

By design, this is the first time that money has been mentioned in a book about stewardship. Too often, stewardship is incorrectly used as a euphemism for money. I don't dare count the times that a fellow pastor has contacted me to ask how I made stewardship work. I do know that too often, once I ask a few questions of the inquiring pastor, it becomes obvious that he is not interested in stewardship but is interested only in increasing the parish offertory collection. Stewardship does not equal money; nevertheless money is certainly part of stewardship.

Some people talk of tithing; others talk about sacrificial giving. I like to talk about percentage giving. Write down your income (if you have to ask gross or net you are missing the point) then write down what you give in charitable giving. Once you have these two numbers you will be able to calculate what percentage of your Treasure you are returning to the Lord. You will probably be surprised by how small the percentage is. The goal is to eventually give 10% of your income to charity. The 10% is frequently broken down this way: 3% to your parish, 2% to the diocese and other religious giving and 5% to civic charitable giving. Once you figure out what percentage of your income you are giving to charity increase it by 1% and do so every year until you reach the goal of 10%. By so doing, you will be certain that you are making a return with increase to the Lord.

Once we understand that charitable giving is part of our making a return with increase to the Lord, we will understand that there are many ways to make a return with increase to the Lord. We need to find time for prayer; likewise we need to find time to reach out to our neighbor. When we find the time to visit a friend who is depressed, we make a return with increase to the Lord. If we find the time to be a coach for Little League, or football or soccer, we make a return to the Lord. The same is true of working at a soup kitchen, a women's shelter or a homeless shelter. These examples of giving Time are offered as example. There are many other ways of reaching out to others that are also ways of making a return to the Lord.

Perhaps an example will help make this point. If you are a parent with adult children you will relate to what I am about to say; if not, then like me, you will have to imagine what I am about to say. Picture parents sitting in a large field house at a graduation ceremony. Imagine, or remember, your daughter or son walking across the stage and receiving her or his diploma. Be in touch with the feelings of pride and satisfaction in your heart. Remember how hard it was to follow the request "to hold your applause until all have received their diploma."

Now let's take apart this experience. Go back to when your child was born, back to the sleepless nights. Remember the first steps, the first words. Remember your child's first experience of going off to school. Call to mind those parent teacher meetings and being told, "She is not working up to her potential." Remember the first time that a curfew was missed. If you dare, remember the sullen look of adolescent angst which greeted your attempts to be a good parent. Remember when he did not make the basketball team or when her first break-up sent her into an emotional tailspin. Remember the whole

40

thing. When your child received that diploma, whether cum laude (with praise) or cum flectu (with tears), your child made a return with increase on the gift of your patient love offered over all those years. Parenting is part of stewardship as is friendship, work, and being a good neighbor. The spirituality of stewardship is inclusive, demanding, and joyful.

STUDY QUESTIONS:

1. How could finding more time for prayer help us maintain proper focus in our lives?

2. Where could you more generously share your Time, Talent, and Treasure?

3. What needs to change so you can more freely "pay forward" God's gifts of Time, Talent, and Treasure?

Chapter VIII

IT IS BAPTISM
THAT MAKES US
STEWARDS / DISCIPLES

You have been taught that when we were baptized
In Christ Jesus we were baptized into his death;
In other words, when we were baptized we went into
the tomb with him and joined him in death,
so that as Christ was raised from the dead by the Father's glory,
we too might live a new life.

Romans 6:3-4

The Second Vatican Council in its decree on the Liturgy *(Sacrosanctum Concillum)* made it clear that over the centuries some features have entered our sacramental celebrations "which have rendered their nature and purpose less clear to the people of today…" (SC 62). In the past fifty years much progress has been made updating the rites that surround our sacramental celebrations; much work still needs to be done.

In the early days of our church, Baptism was an adult experience. When someone heard of the "Good News of salvation offered in the person of Christ Jesus" and wished to become a follower she presented herself for Baptism. The early church, as does

43

the contemporary church, took seriously the mandate Jesus gave at the end of Matthew's gospel: "Go, therefore, make disciples of all the nations; baptize them in the name of the Father and of the Son and of the Holy Spirit, and teach them to observe all the commands I gave you. And know that I am with you always; yes, to the end of time." (Matt. 28:16-20)

It is unclear when the baptism of infants entered into the Catholic Church. It would appear that the practice became the norm sometime during the 4th century and that St. Augustine and his teaching on original sin were instrumental in this change. Oddly enough, St. Augustine, the first-born child of a pagan father and a Christian mother, was not baptized as a child. His baptism took place 387 CE at the age of 33.

It was Augustine's teaching on original sin that ushered in what became, in the Catholic tradition, the universal practice of infant baptism and the first change in our understanding of the sacrament of Baptism. In the early Church, Baptism "in the name of the Father and the Son and the Holy Spirit" celebrated a conversion from paganism or Judaism to Christianity. With the introduction of original sin, Baptism took on the added meaning of forgiveness of the sin inherited from Adam and Eve. Over time, as the Church continued to grow, infant Baptism became the norm and the aspect of conversion was pushed from the center of understanding this sacrament to its periphery. With this evolution, Baptism became a passive rather than an active experience.

Baptism is the pre-eminent sacrament of initiation; it is the gate that opens for us access to the other six sacraments. It is the sacrament that unites all believers. Not every believer receives Confirmation, not every believer receives Eucharist, not every believer receives Reconciliation, Marriage, Holy Orders, or the Anointing of the Sick but every believer receives Baptism. Even more than Eucharist, Baptism is the sacrament of unity. As the

Baltimore Catechism of my youth taught, in Baptism "we become the sons and daughters of God and heirs to the Kingdom of Heaven." How we live and interact with each other as sons and daughters in the family of God's love gets played out in the context of the other six sacraments but we must never forget that it is Baptism that makes us one.

Here is a story that I hope will bring home the importance of what really happens to us at Baptism: A woman traveling by train arrives at the track 4 platform. At the far end of the platform she sees a large crate with a dog inside. She seeks out the stationmaster and asks why the dog is sitting in a crate on the platform. The stationmaster tells her that the dog ate his address label and now no one knows where the dog was going! In many ways, this is what has happened to the baptized in today's church. We did not eat the address label given to us at our Baptism but history and the institution certainly did.

How this happened is beyond the scope of this book but this history must be sketched out here if we are to rediscover the gift that God, not the Church, gave us at Baptism.

In the early church there was only the People of God. All were united; all had different charisms. The services performed by the baptized were different but they were not yet considered inferior or superior. Just read 1 Corinthians 12:4-11, "There is a variety of gifts but always the same Spirit; there are all sorts of service to be done, but always the same Lord; working in all sorts of different ways in different people, it is the same God who is working in all of them. The particular way in which the Spirit is given to each person is for a good purpose. One may have the gift of preaching with wisdom given him by the Spirit; another may have the gift of preaching instruction given him by the same Spirit; and another the gift of faith given by the same Spirit; another again the gift of healing, through this one Spirit; one, the power of miracles; another,

45

prophecy; another the gift of recognizing spirits; another the gift of tongues and another the ability to interpret them. All these are the work of one and the same Spirit, who distributes different gifts to different people as he chooses."

We know that as the early church evolved, the Apostles recognized the need for believers to be appointed to serve the needs of the poor and widowed: "About this time, when the number of disciples was increasing, the Hellenists made a complaint against the Hebrews: in the daily distribution their own widows were being overlooked. So the Twelve called a full meeting of the disciples and addressed them, 'It would not be right for us to neglect the word of God so as to give out food, you, brothers, must select from among yourselves seven men of good reputation, filled with the Spirit and with wisdom; we will hand over this duty to them and continue to devote ourselves to prayer and to the service of the word.' The whole assembly approved of this proposal..." (Acts 6:1-5). Thus began the ministry of deacons. The early Church was now made up of apostles, deacons and disciples. Nevertheless the gifts given to each group were still seen as different rather than superior or inferior.

As the early Church continued to grow there became a need for still another form of ministry—presbyter or priest. This last group was necessary if the Eucharist was to be more readily available to the disciples. With the addition of presbyter the Church was now made up of four different groups: Apostles (bishops), presbyters (priests), deacons and disciples (laity) but the understanding of the gifts specific to each group was still that of different rather than inferior or superior. Unfortunately, as the Church continued to evolve, the gifts given to each group were seen as superior or inferior and the unity of the Baptized was lost as the clergy were perceived as or were presented as superior and the laity as inferior members of the Church. As George Wilson says in his powerful little book, *Clericalism: The Death of the Priesthood,* "Once there was a clergy and a laity it was only a matter of time before superior and inferior membership entered the scene." This split-level membership continued over time until we ended up with what one author called "The Father knows best Church." In that Church, the laity was assigned and eventually gladly accepted passive membership! The role of the laity was to pray, pay, and obey!

When St. John XXIII called his brother bishops together for the Second Vatican Council in 1962, one of the most important concepts the Holy Spirit led the bishops to consider was how to rediscover the proper place of the laity, the baptized, in the life of our Church. The bishops responded to this invitation in many of the documents and decrees of the Council. In the decree on the Missionary activity of the Church *Ad Gentes* they wrote, "The Church has not been truly established, and is not yet fully alive, nor is it a perfect sign of Christ among men, unless there exists a laity worthy of the name working along with the hierarchy. For the gospel cannot be deeply imprinted on the talents, life and work of any people without the active presence of laymen. Therefore, even in the very founding of a Church, the greatest attention is to be paid to raising up a mature Christian laity." (AG 21)

In the Council's constitution on the Church *Lumen Gentium* they wrote, "The term laity is here understood to mean all the faithful except those in holy orders and those in a religious state sanctioned by the church. These faithful are by baptism made one body with Christ and are established among the People of God." (LG 31) This quote is both helpful and hurtful—helpful because it recognizes that it is Baptism that establishes us as the People of God; hurtful because it continues the erroneous definition of laity as those who are "not clergy."

It will take a long time for the superior/inferior and clergy/laity two-tiered membership assumptions to be driven out of our Church but the Council at least set the Church on the right road. There are signs of hope as well as signs of discouragement in the progress we are making. Pope Francis is one of the most hopeful signs that progress is once again on the ascendency. He has both spoken and acted in accordance with this insight from his Apostolic Exhortation, *Evangelii Gaudium*, "In virtue of their Baptism, all the members of the People of God have become missionary disciples (Matt. 28:29). All the baptized, whatever their position in the Church or their level of instruction in the faith, are agents of evangelization, and it would be insufficient to envision a plan of evangelization to be carried out by professionals while the rest of the faithful would simply be passive recipients. The new evangelization calls for personal involvement on the part of each of the baptized." (EG 120)

I would like to share with you a story that gives me hope that the laity will soon come of age in our Church. It is a humorous story that involved my father. He was a faithful Catholic. He went to Sunday Mass, always! He went to the Holy Name Society Communion breakfast once a year. He signed up for adoration at 3 am on the night that bridged Holy Thursday and Good Friday. He said his prayers and obeyed the rules. He worked hard at saving his soul. He was appointed once to a term on the parish council; when his term was up they did not invite him to serve a second term. My dad was a civil engineer and, as such, was asked to serve on a committee formed to reconfigure his parish church so that there would be four rather than two communion stations at Sunday Mass. The committee met a few times and came up with options, "A," "B," and "C" with the unanimous recommendation that option "C" be implemented. A few weeks later, my father received a call from the priest who had formed the committee. He informed my father that option "A" would be implemented. My father asked why and the priest said because he wanted option "A". When my father pointed out to him, once again, that option "A" was a flawed design, the priest got exasperated and blurted out, "That's what's wrong with the Church today! Why don't you just do what the priest tells you?" My father was a wonderful man and, in truth, a man of few words but he had had enough so he said, "Father, they ordained my boy, Joe, and, trust me, he got no smarter in the process." I was never so proud of him as when he told me that story. What my father was saying was there are a lot of smart people in the Church and not all of them or even most of them are ordained. He was acting on the power given to him at Baptism. Unfortunately, my father's and the rest of the committee's attempt to live out the power given to them at Baptism was thwarted; option "A" was foisted on the people. To this day it still does not work well.

We have a lot of work to do to end the clerical/lay divide in our Church. The title of the American Bishops' Pastoral letter, *Stewardship: A Disciple's Response*, and its content helps to point out the road to recovery because it is clear that the title could have been, Stewardship: The Response of the Baptized.

STUDY QUESTIONS:

1. How has the concept of superior/inferior membership in the Church affected your active participation in the life of your parish?

2. As a layperson, how can you help your pastor respect your Baptismal call?

3. As a priest, how can you be more open to helping the Baptized to share in ministry?

Chapter IX

CONFIRMATION, THE GIFT THAT KEEPS GIVING

Confirmation symbolizes the human spirit
of faith, hope, and love, and continues to initiate
into the Christian community by "sealing" Christians
with the gifts of the Holy Spirit, strengthening them
to live their faith in the world.

Thomas Groome
What Makes Us Catholic

*L*ike Baptism, Confirmation has wandered from its original meaning. It is not clear at the beginning of the Church if there was a distinction between Baptism and Confirmation. It seems in the beginning that Baptism and Confirmation were two distinct acts within one Sacrament. Nevertheless in Acts 8:14-17, we are told, "When the Apostles in Jerusalem heard that Samaria had accepted the word of God, they sent Peter and John to them, and they went down there, and prayed for the Samaritans to receive the Holy Spirit, for as yet he had not come down on any of them: they had only been baptized in the name of the Lord Jesus. They laid hands on them, and they received the Holy Spirit." Clearly this quote shows that there was occasionally a separation in the baptism with water and the gift of the Spirit. Recall this event from Acts 19:1-7,

"While Apollos was in Corinth, Paul made his way overland as far as Ephesus, where he found a number of disciples. When he asked, 'Did you receive the Holy Spirit when you became believers?' they answered, 'No, we were never told there was such a thing as a Holy Spirit.' 'Then how were you baptized?' he asked. 'With John's baptism,' they replied. 'John's baptism,' said Paul 'was a baptism of repentance; but he insisted that the people should believe in the one who was to come after him—in other words Jesus.' When they heard this, they were baptized in the name of the Lord Jesus, and the moment Paul laid hands on them the Holy Spirit came down on them and they began to speak with tongues and prophesy." In this passage, we are reminded that the baptism of Jesus replaces all other baptisms and that "the laying on of hands by one of the apostles" was part of Baptism.

While it is fascinating that the Church of the East has kept Baptism, Confirmation, and Eucharist together as the Sacraments of Initiation and the Church of the West has separated them, the unraveling of those two traditions is far beyond the scope of this book. For now, it will hopefully be sufficient to say that it would be wonderful if the Roman Church would act on the suggestion of Benedict XVI in his 2007 Apostolic Exhortation *Sacramentum Caritatis* and return to the original order of the Sacraments of Initiation.

The present order for the reception of the Sacraments in the Roman Catholic Church is not historically justifiable. There are three sacraments of initiation—Baptism, Confirmation, and Eucharist and four sacraments of living—Marriage, Holy Orders, Reconciliation and the Anointing of the Sick. Ideally believers should receive the three sacraments of initiation in order and then the other four sacraments when appropriate. Presently the order of the sacraments for most believers is Baptism, Reconciliation, Eucharist, and Confirmation. Reconciliation before Eucharist is even required by Canon Law and many diocesan regulations. However, that does not mean that the law or regulations are theologically or historically correct. Indeed the law and the regulations confuse the true meaning of both Reconciliation and Eucharist.

Confirmation, like most of the sacraments, has had both an interesting and confusing evolution. As mentioned above, the Second Vatican Council encouraged a return to the original meaning of the sacraments so that historically induced confusion could be removed. This is certainly the case with Confirmation. In the span of my life, the age for reception of Confirmation has been mercurial to say the least. My two older brothers were confirmed together. One was in the fifth grade, the other was in the fourth grade. I was confirmed in the fourth grade at the age of nine. I am not sure how old my younger brother was when he was confirmed. But somewhere after I was confirmed the age for Confirmation began to climb. When I was in active parish ministry, the age was fifteen or sixteen and Confirmation had been transformed into both an opportunity to renew the Baptismal promises made for us by our parents and godparents and a ritual of passage as an adult in the Church. Confirmation had morphed into kind of Bar or Bat Mitzvah! Perhaps the Church needs to develop such a ritual but it should not do so at the expense of the real meaning of Confirmation.

What then is the sacrament of Confirmation and how is it related to the spirituality of stewardship in our lives of faith? The Baltimore Catechism simply states, "Confirmation is a sacrament through which we receive the Holy Ghost to make us strong and perfect Christians as soldiers of Jesus Christ." The Catechism of the Catholic Church gives a more developed definition, "For by the sacrament of Confirmation, [the baptized] are more perfectly bound to the Church and are enriched with a special strength of the Holy Spirit. Hence they are, as true witnesses of Christ, more strictly obliged to spread and defend the faith by word and deed."

(1285). To put it another way: in Confirmation the baptized are reminded of their call to be disciples and according to the bishops' pastoral letter stewardship is a disciple's response.

All sacraments contain the gift of God's presence appropriate to each sacrament's meaning. Confirmation is the most gift-laden sacrament. Let us listen, once again, to the prayer said by the bishop at Confirmation, "My dear friends: in Baptism God our Father gave the new birth of eternal life to his chosen sons and daughters. Let us pray to our Father that he will pour out the Holy Spirit to strengthen his sons and daughters with his gifts and anoint them to be more like Christ, the Son of God." After a pause during which time all present pray for those about to be confirmed, the bishop continues, "All powerful God, Father of our Lord Jesus Christ by water and the Holy Spirit you freed your sons and daughters from sin and gave them new life. Send your Holy Spirit upon them to be their helper and guide. Give them the spirit of Wisdom and Understanding, the Spirit of Right Judgment and Courage, the Spirit of Knowledge and Reverence. Fill them with the Spirit of Wonder and Awe in your presence, through Christ our Lord. Amen."

Confirmation gives to all who receive it the seven gifts of the Holy Spirit: Wisdom, Understanding, Right Judgment, Courage, Knowledge, Reverence, and Wonder and Awe. Surely these gifts are essential to embracing the spirituality of stewardship. They must, as stewardship requires, be received gratefully, developed responsibly, shared lovingly with others, and returned to God with growth.

I will end this chapter with a reflection on the meaning of each of these gifts and its implications for all good stewards.

WISDOM: We are not alone on the journey of faith. We are blessed with the lived experience of all those who have gone before us on the journey of faith. We have at our disposal the rich history of the

54

teachings and traditions of our Church and our elders. The light of their truth lights our path as we live out the gift of faith given to us in Baptism and enriched by Confirmation.

UNDERSTANDING: This gift requires a bit of nuance. Our faith is filled with mystery. If understanding removes all mystery then there is no need for faith. God's love for us is a mystery that we will never be able to totally understand. That Jesus took on our human condition is a mystery. That Jesus suffered and died for us is a mystery. We will never understand the mystery of God's love but we can better understand that it is a mystery.

RIGHT JUDGMENT: A gift we all need. In the struggle to live better lives we come upon many crossroads. God, through the Holy Spirit, is with us to help us make right decisions. He does not force us to make good decisions because that would destroy free will but He is there to help us if we are willing to call upon Him.

COURAGE: To be a believer, to be a disciple, to be a good steward requires courage. Left to our own resources we would frequently fail to stand up for our faith. When we waiver, as we all do, God is there to support and encourage us to do what we know is right.

KNOWLEDGE: The resources are all there. The Church, The People of God, offers us instruction. We can learn to be better Christians. We learn from those who teach us. We learn from our life experiences. The Holy Spirit guides us so that we can better know what Scripture and tradition has to say.

REVERENCE: This is a gift that is truly underdeveloped in our world. Reverence, respect for the dignity that is the birthright of each individual, is absent from so many aspects of our lives. In the categories

55

made famous by Martin Buber, reverence helps us discover the "I—Thou" relationship God has fashioned with us and work toward building the same relationship with all of our sisters and brothers in the human family.

WONDER AND AWE: This last gift used to be called "Fear of the Lord" which only causes confusion. Thankfully, it has been changed to "wonder and awe in the presence of God." Many of us have spent too many years being afraid of God. This gift helps us see the wonder of God in all creation and be in awe because God has so lavishly sprinkled our world with the signs of His presence.

There is a tendency to treat the sacraments as static rather than dynamic events. We are in the habit of saying, "I was baptized and I was confirmed" as if they were past events or milestones on our journey of faith. We would be better off and better stewards if we would begin to say and think, "I am being baptized. I am being confirmed." That way each day can be seen as an invitation to renew and respond more fully to the gift of faith and the gifts of the Holy Spirit and become not just good stewards but better stewards of all God's gifts.

STUDY QUESTIONS:

1. The Catechism of the Catholic teaches that in Confirmation the baptized are more perfectly bound to the church and are enriched with a special strength of the Holy Spirit. How can that understanding of Confirmation take root in your life?

2. How does the spirit of Wonder and Awe in God's presence manifest itself in your life?

3. What gift of the Holy Spirit do you need to develop more fully?

Chapter X

EUCHARIST: LET US GIVE THANKS TO THE LORD, OUR GOD

This is what we express when we take bread and wine in thanksgiving.
We do not eat bread to still our hunger
or drink wine to quench our thirst.
We eat just a little bit of bread and drink a little bit of wine,
in the realization that God's presence is the presence
of the one who came, but is still to come;
who touched our hearts but has not yet taken all our sadness away.

Henri Nouwen
Out of Solitude

Baptism makes us disciples with both a mission and a ministry; Confirmation seals us with the seven-fold gifts of the Holy Spirit. Eucharist feeds our body, mind, and spirit; it motivates us to live our faith to its fullness. We eat the bread and drink the wine to make sure that we do not forget the love that motivated Jesus to suffer and die for us; to make sure that we never forget that his love was rewarded when his father called him back to life and changed human history forever! Eucharist is the stewardship sacrament par excellence.

Without a grateful heart, Eucharist cannot be fully experienced. As we are painfully aware, attendance at Sunday Mass is at an all-time low. The explanations for the scandalous decline in Mass attendance are many and it is doubtful that any one explanation can explain fully why participation in the Eucharist on Sunday fails to motivate so many people.

There are some who believe that when the liturgy was no longer celebrated in Latin that we lost our sense of mystery. Once the mystery was gone, people began to drift away. While it cannot be disputed that the beginning of the drop in attendance at Sunday Mass began about the same time that English was introduced most would agree that the relationship is coincidental rather than causal.

Others believe that the drop in Mass attendance is the result of secularism. When I was a young boy all of Sunday but especially Sunday morning was reserved for church. There was no shopping because all the stores were closed. There were no Sunday morning road races, no soccer matches, and no football games. Sunday morning was for Church. Obviously this is no longer the case. For too many folks Sunday is the only day they do not work. Sunday is now seen as personal time for those who work too long and too hard. Religion now has to compete with an ever-increasing number of opportunities on Sunday and we are not winning the battle.

Some folks were driven away from Church as a reaction to the sexual abuse scandal that is ongoing in our Church. Some think that as believers get better educated their need for church wanes. Still others insist that the new English translation of the Mass, which is stilted and overly formal, has added to the problem of declining participation in Sunday Mass. In addition to all of these contributing factors is the reality that more and more people do not believe that missing Mass on Sunday is a sin. Whatever the real reason or reasons, no one can deny that we have a problem and we need to find a solution.

I firmly believe that the spirituality of stewardship provides a major solution to the problem of declining Sunday Mass attendance. Eucharist means thanksgiving and the first step on the road to becoming a good steward is "To receive God's gifts gratefully." If we can enrich the "attitude of gratitude" in our lives and in the lives of the people we love then we will be on the road to recovery. Once we rediscover that "everything we have is a gift from God" then we will be forever vigilant in our search for ways to thank God for all that he has given us. There is no better way to thank God than to gather with our fellow believers, admit our sinfulness, give glory to God, open our minds and hearts to the Word of God proclaimed, offer our gifts, pray together for those gifts to be transformed into the Body and Blood of Christ, receive communion and then be sent forth to a waiting world with the message that God gives us the gift of his love.

The Second Vatican Council, in its decree on the Liturgy, reminds us "liturgy is the summit towards which the activity of the Church is directed; at the same time it is the fountain from which all her power flows." (SC 10). It has been fifty years since the Council issued its first decree on the liturgy. Much has been done to restore liturgy to its central role in the life of the Church. More remains to be done so that the vision of "full, active, and conscious" participation in the Mass becomes the norm rather than the exception.

It is impossible to actively join in the celebration of the Mass and not have our hearts filled with gratitude. Whenever we gather to celebrate the Mass, we come to give thanks to God for all his gifts and a miracle happens. We come to give thanks, we receive more gifts, and we go forth with even more for which to be thankful.

The best way to explore the miracle, mystery of the Eucharist, is to take part in an extended meditation of just what happens when we gather to break bread as the People of God.

The first thing we do after the entrance procession is to sign ourselves in the name of the Father, and the Son, and the Holy Spirit. The cross is our sign of contradiction. It tells us of God's Trinitarian love by reminding us that Jesus' love led him to suffer and die for us. We should never make the sign of the cross without realizing our need to thank God for sending Jesus to be our savior!

Next we pause to call to mind our sins. We are sinners; we need God's mercy. Every time we gather to celebrate the Mass, God offers us forgiveness. We are invited to thank God for his prodigal forgiveness.

The forgiveness of our sins leads us to say, "Glory to God!" As we sing the Gloria we pray, "we give you thanks for your great glory." This is the first, but certainly not the last time, we will say or hear the word "thanks" in the celebration of the Mass.

Now we sit to hear the readings from scripture that can both challenge and comfort us on our journey of faith. After the first reading, what do we say? "Thanks be to God!" After the second reading, what do we say? "Thanks be to God!" Now we stand to hear the Gospel and what do we say when it is finished? "Praise to you, Lord Jesus Christ!" Praise is but another way of saying "Thank You."

After the homily, the Creed and the General Intercessions the activity of the gathered people changes. We move from the Liturgy of the Word to the Liturgy of the Eucharist. What is the first thing we do? We bring the gifts of bread and wine to the altar. The priest receives the gifts and individually holds them up and reminds us "through your goodness we have this bread to offer" and "through your goodness we have this wine to offer." There is no spoken response to these prayers but our hearts should say, "Thanks be to God."

Next comes the Eucharistic prayer. Our threefold versical and response concludes with "Let us give thanks to the Lord, our

God." We used to respond, "It is right and just to give God thanks and praise." I prefer the older translation because we got to say "thanks" out loud. For now, "It is right and just" will have to suffice.

Now the priest reminds us of what Jesus said and did at the Last Supper. It is the simple words of a man who knew he was soon to die but was determined to find a way to remain with us. "He took the bread and gave you thanks…" "He took the chalice, again he gave you thanks." This is why we call it Eucharist because Jesus gave thanks! We are called and reminded to do the same.

The Eucharistic prayer ends and we prepare for communion. We set aside our individuality and call upon God as "Our Father." We exchange the sign of peace. We join the centurion in Scripture not by expressing our unworthiness but professing our belief that God has the power to transform our lives and make them better, "say but the word and my soul will be healed." Then we come forward not just to receive the body and blood of Christ but also to become what we receive. We are now the body and blood of Christ. Our hearts are filled with gratitude.

One final prayer and a blessing, then "The Mass is ended. Go in Peace." Together we all proclaim, "Thanks be to God!" As a child my "Thanks be to God" was really "Thank God this is over." As an adult it is "Thanks be to God for the mystery of his love. Thanks be to God for this gathering together. Thanks be to God for this wonderful sacrament. Thanks be to God that I am now sent into the world to continue the transformation."

We should come away from the Eucharist renewed in our faith and reminded of the call to be his disciples, the stewards of all God has given us.

STUDY QUESTION:

1. How can the "attitude of gratitude" insure that you remain faithful to Sunday liturgy?

2. In what ways could you be more active in your celebration of Mass?

3. What are some ways that the liturgy inspires you to continue the transformation of our world?

Chapter XI

RECONCILIATION, THE ANOINTING OF THE SICK, MARRIAGE, AND HOLY ORDERS: FOUR MORE GIFTS FROM GOD

A sacrament is a festive action
in which Christians assemble to celebrate
their lived experience and to call to heart
their common story.
The action is a symbol of God's care for us in Christ.
Enacting the symbol brings us closer to one another
in the church and to the Lord who is there for us.

Tad Guzie
The Book of Sacramental Basics

J remember reading somewhere that when a book is being written it takes on a life of its own. Once I read it; now I believe it. This chapter was not in my original outline. However as the book evolved, as the notion of stewardship as a spirituality developed, and after I had taken the time to anchor stewardship in the three sacraments of Initiation, it seemed necessary to add this chapter dealing with how stewardship is nourished in the remaining four

Sacraments—Reconciliation, Anointing of the Sick, Marriage and Holy Orders.

Catholics are a sacramental people; our entire life is ordered around the sacraments. Baptism, Confirmation, and Holy Orders are sacraments that are performed once but lived every day of our lives. Marriage for the vast majority of those who celebrate it is a once in a lifetime sacrament. Because sometimes "death does do us part" a small percentage of people get to celebrate marriage more than once. Eucharist is celebrated over and over again. Reconciliation used to be celebrated much more frequently than is presently the case for most Catholics. Finally, the Anointing of the Sick can be celebrated as often as needed but most believers never celebrate it at all. This chapter will offer a brief description on how each of these four Sacraments— the two sacraments of healing (Reconciliation and the Anointing of the Sick) and the two sacraments of living (Marriage and Holy Orders)—are gifts from God that need to be received gratefully, developed responsibly, lovingly shared with others, and returned to God with increase.

SACRAMENTS OF HEALING

RECONCILIATION: People always look at me oddly when I tell them that Reconciliation is one of my favorite sacraments. It is actually a close second to Eucharist, which is my favorite sacrament. I love Reconciliation on both sides of the kneeler. I love being the sign of God's forgiveness as a priest hearing confession and I love being the penitent who receives God's loving forgiveness. Reconciliation proves for me that Jesus took on our human condition and although he was free from sin he recognized the reality of human sinfulness and humanity's ongoing need for forgiveness. The Sacrament of Reconciliation has had a wild journey through the history of the Church. In the early days of the Church (up until the Council of Carthage 298 CE), what we used to call confession could be celebrated only once in a lifetime. Sometime in the 6th century, when Irish monks set about re-Christianizing Europe, they brought with them what we call private confession. In the Middle Ages one of the Precepts of the Church was to go to confession once a year. At the beginning of the 20th century, Pope Pius X moved the age for the reception of First Communion from twelve or thirteen years old to seven years of age. Confession before First Communion was required. It is difficult for us to imagine but Pius X was known as the "Pope of frequent communion." For a number of reasons by the beginning of the 20th century it was not the norm for people to receive communion every time they went to Mass. As a matter of fact, there is a Precept of the Church, now no longer relevant, that requires people to receive Communion once a year during the Easter Season.

So in the early church confession could be celebrated only once; in the Church just prior to the Second Vatican Council confession was required prior to the reception of Communion. That is quite an evolution. To add to the confusion surrounding this wonderful sacrament, we kept changing its name. When I was growing up, we used to say, "I'm going to Confession." Then I was told that the sacrament was no longer called Confession; now it was called the Sacrament of Penance. Then, after the reforms of the Second Vatican Council, it was called Reconciliation. I would like to suggest one last name change for this sacrament. Let's just call it Forgiveness. Why? Well for starters everyone knows what forgiveness means and very few know what reconciliation means. Also I think it would be great for every church to have a Forgiveness Room rather than a Reconciliation Room.

Forgiveness is God's gift to us as we struggle to let faith guide our life choices. I have never met a believer who has not strayed from the right path. All of us have failed; all of us have sinned. All of us need to experience the loving forgiveness of our God.

John 3:16 is frequently called the gospel in miniature. That is why at every major sporting event someone will hold up a sign that says John 3:16. I'm not sure how many people see those signs and run to their Bible to look up the reference: "Yes, God loved the world so much that he gave his only Son so that everyone who believes in him may not be lost but may have eternal life." With no disrespect to John 3:16, I would like to suggest another version of the gospel in miniature. The four Gospels are a compilation of stories of Jesus encountering people who have lost their way—the woman at the well with five husbands, Zacchaeus, the tax collector and cheat, the woman caught in adultery, the good thief, Peter, who denied him three times, the prodigal son and the older brother, etc. Jesus says to each of them, "I don't care where you have been; I don't care what you have done. I love you. I forgive you and I set you free." For me that is the Gospel in miniature. God knows we cannot change the past. What we've done, we've done. When we ask for forgiveness in the here and now, God loves us and forgives us. Because of God's love and forgiveness, we are set free to become the people God calls us to be!

Just as there are different levels of wandering from the path of faith, so there are different levels of forgiveness. Sometimes a sincere act of contrition will suffice. On other occasions, the penitential rite at the beginning of Mass where we are invited to call to mind our sins and then the priest prays, "May Almighty God have mercy on us, forgive us our sins and lead us to eternal life," will be the level of forgiveness we need. There will unfortunately be times when we wander far from the way of truth and we will want and need to celebrate the sacramental forgiveness.

Forgiveness, at whatever level appropriate considering our level of offense, is a gift from God. As good stewards we need to receive the gift of forgiveness with gratitude, let that forgiveness heal us, share that healing with others, and say "Thank You" to God by living better lives.

THE ANOINTING OF THE SICK: Like Reconciliation, this sacrament has an interesting history. All the sacraments are rooted in the Bible but no sacrament is more clearly stated or described in scripture than the Anointing of the Sick. The opening instruction in the ritual, Pastoral Care of the Sick, in the section for the celebration of the Anointing Outside of Mass, contains this quote from James 4:14-15: "Are there any who are sick among you? Let them send for the priests of the Church, and let the priests pray over them, anointing them with oil in the name of the Lord; and the prayer of faith will save the sick person, and the Lord will raise them up; and if they have committed any sins, their sins will be forgiven them." That the prayer urges that the sick person send for the "priests" rather than the "priest" is a bit curious. Of the most popular English translations of the Bible, only the much older Douay Rheims uses "priests." The New Revised Standard Version, the Revised Standard Version and the Jerusalem Bible use the word "elders." The New American Bible uses the word "presbyters." Either of which is probably more accurate and would explain the use of a plural noun but that is an issue best left for others to probe.

The above quote from James 4:14-15 and this quote from Mark 6:13: "So they set off to preach repentance; and they cast out many devils, and anointed many sick people with oil and cured them," shows that what we know today as the Anointing of the Sick has biblical roots. As the sacrament evolved, the emphasis of the sick being anointed got lost and the focus shifted to the dying. The various names for this sacrament reflect that change of focus. Sometimes it was called "The Last Rites"; other times it was called "Extreme Unction." Either title adds a somber gravity to the sacrament that was not conducive to a proper understanding of the sacrament. Fortunately the 1983 revised ritual calls this sacrament The Anointing of the Sick, which hopefully will lead to a more accurate understanding of this sacrament. Anyone actively involved in parish ministry knows that there is still considerable misunderstanding surrounding this healing sacrament.

I remember very clearly one of the first times I celebrated the Anointing of the Sick. More clearly one of the first times I attempted to celebrate the Anointing of the Sick. I was called to a house a few blocks from the rectory. The family was encamped in the kitchen well stocked with coffee and pastry. Al, the one who needed to be anointed, was in a hospital bed in the living room. The family offered me something to eat but would not let me into the living room. Finally they told me that "if their father sees the priest in his living room" then he would be scared and know he was dying. I tried to explain that he probably knew that his days were numbered since he was in a hospital bed in his living room but they were not listening. I returned to the rectory and complained to my pastor, who was a very good priest who taught me how to be more pastoral in my ministry. He told me "old ways" are hard to change. He also predicted that the family would come pounding at the rectory door at 2:30 some morning requesting Al's anointing. He was off by an hour; he conveniently slept through the pounding on the door. I got dressed and went to the home where Al was no longer capable of being scared by the priest in his living room. I anointed him conditionally and went home knowing that a true sacramental experience had been missed. Sadly some of that misunderstanding of the Anointing of the Sick still persists.

Thankfully some progress has been made. I remember another sacramental experience that was not missed. Her name was Inez, her birthday was July 4, and every year she would host a joint celebration of her birthday and our country's freedom. Inez was a very faithful member of our parish and had helped establish the Stephen Ministry program in our parish. She had cancer. She refused to say she was dying of cancer; she insisted on saying she was living with cancer. When her last birthday celebration was approaching she asked me if I would anoint her at her party with her family and friends all present.

I said I would and so began what, to this day, is one of the most powerful celebrations of the Anointing of the Sick I have ever experienced. At her last 4th of July celebration, between the hot dogs and hamburgers, surrounded by pasta salad and potato salad and just before dessert, we gathered around, sang songs, proclaimed Scripture, laid on hands, anointed a fellow believer and prayed, "Lord Jesus Christ, you chose to share our human nature, to redeem all people, and to heal the sick. Look with compassion upon your servant whom we have anointed in your name with this holy oil for healing of her body and spirit. Support her with your power, comfort her with your protection, and give her the strength to fight against evil. Since you have given her a share in your own passion, help her find hope in suffering, for you are Lord forever and ever. Amen!" I'm not sure if what happened in her back yard that day was done completely by the book but I do know that a sacramental experience was certainly not missed.

I have no idea how many people I have anointed. I know that I have been anointed once. All anointings are similar and all are different. Some are done with family and friends present; some are done in eerie solitude. But every celebration is done in the context of the Christian community. As the believing community grows in its understanding of this sacrament, it is the exception not the rule for a priest to be called to the hospital in the middle of the night. Nevertheless, it still happens. I remember receiving a call one night from a man who was thousands of miles away. He told me that the local hospital had just called him to inform him that his brother had passed away. Apologetically he asked if I could go to the hospital and say a prayer for his brother. I did. When I got to the hospital a nurse's aide led me to a very barren room—there was just a hospital bed with a light on the headboard and a body with a sheet pulled over his head. I asked the nurse's aide if she wanted to stay while I said some prayers. She declined. I don't remember if I anointed the brother provisionally or

71

if I just said the prayer for the dead. I do remember all the prayers saying "we" even though there was just me and the corpse in the room yet I did not feel alone. I was united with a grieving brother half a country away. I was supported by the community of faith that I was called to serve. The communion of saints and the community of the faithful became very real for me that evening.

Healing is a gift from God. Being part of the family that can say, "Our Farther," being brothers and sisters in the Lord are gifts.

We need to receive God's healing, develop the gift of community with others, welcome the strangers in our midst and one day take our seat at the banquet of God's love in the Kingdom of Heaven.

SACRAMENTS OF LIVING

MARRIAGE: It took a long time for the Catholic Church to consider marriage a sacrament. Marriage in some form or other has been around since the beginning of human history. Marriage is frequently mentioned throughout the Bible. Nevertheless, there was no clear notion of marriage as a sacrament in the church until the 12th century. The Church began to take an active interest in marriage only as the Roman Empire began to collapse and someone needed to regulate marriage for the good of society, which partially explains why even today the Church still struggles to view marriage in a spiritual rather than legalistic way. The Council of Trent (1545-1563) officially declared marriage to be one of the seven sacraments as a response to the Protestant Reformation's efforts to reduce the number of sacraments to two. Once again, we have a sacrament with an interesting history.

If, as was stated above, the biblical foundations for the Anointing of the Sick are the most obvious, then it should be stated here that the biblical foundations for Marriage as a sacrament are the most vague. That Jesus went to the wedding feast at Cana is used by some as the scriptural foundation for marriage as a sacrament. Others refer to Ephesians 5:21-33 in which we are told, "For this reason, a man must leave his father and mother and be joined to his wife, and the two will become one body. This mystery has many implications; but I am saying it applies to Christ and the Church." Perhaps it would be best to say that the scriptural foundations for marriage as a sacrament are tenuous but sufficient.

Marriage is different from the other six sacraments in two very distinct ways. The sign of Baptism is water, the sign of Confirmation is oil, the sign of Eucharist is the bread and wine, the sign for Anointing of the Sick is oil, the sign for Reconciliation is the imposition of hands and the words of absolution, and the sign for Holy Orders is the imposition of the bishop's hands. What is the sign of Marriage? It is not the vows nor is it the rings. The sign of Marriage is the two people. Marriage is the only sacrament that has people as its sign. That is one difference. The other difference is that Marriage is the only sacrament that is not celebrated by a bishop or a priest. The bride and the groom are the celebrants of Marriage; the priest is but the official witness of the Church. Marriage then is the most personal of the sacraments. It is the only sacrament that is lived in relationship; it is the most difficult and challenging of the seven.

What then are the man and the woman, the bride and the groom, signs of in this most personal sacrament? Love certainly but more than the love they have for each other. They pledge to become signs of God's love for all people. God's all-enduring love, God's never-failing love! And our world is in desperate need of signs of God's love.

Marriage is the vocation that is shared by the largest number of the baptized. Marriage is where the gift of faith is lived. Married couples have a wonderful opportunity to live the spirituality of stewardship in loving relationship. Imagine the enduring power that would emerge if at the beginning of each and every day husbands and wives would remember that they are gifts to and for each other. That their

73

love is a gift. That as husband and wife they are privileged to join with God, the Creator, in bringing new life into the world. That each day is an opportunity to develop and enrich their love for each other and for their children. That they have the opportunity to share the gift and power of their love with everyone they meet. Finally when death ends their sacramental relationship the world around them is a more loving place. What more could a faithful disciple and steward hope to achieve?

HOLY ORDERS: The evolution of "priesthood" in the early Church is fairly uncomplicated. The Apostles were seen as what we now call bishops. Next came deacons, who were assigned to assist with some of the demands being made. "The presence of deacons in the early church is confirmed by the list of attributes that deacons should have. (1 Timothy 3:8-13) The office of "priest" as we now understand it is not present in the New Testament and was the last of the three stages of Holy Orders (Bishop, Priest and Deacon) to be identified. The office of "presbyter" (priest), like the office of deacon, was established because of the rapid growth of the early church. The ordinary priesthood was established as a way of offering the ministry of the Apostles (bishops) especially Baptism and the "breaking of the bread" (Eucharist) to more and more people. What is most important in our consideration of Holy Orders and the spirituality of stewardship is that bishops, priests, and deacons exist to serve the needs of the baptized. Unfortunately, too often it seems like the baptized exist to serve the needs of the ordained (cf. Chapter VIII). We are very fortunate, at the present time, to have Pope Francis reminding us frequently of the dangers of clericalism and the need for a renewed vision of service that is the true ministry of bishops, priests, and deacons. The Church needs to be open to receiving the gift of service from those who are ordained. The laity needs to work at finding their voice in speaking the truth to the ordained so that the relationships between the ordained and the baptized will become healthier and more functional. When this happens then the People of God will be able to share the gifts of the Church more fully with all people. Then the Kingdom of God will truly come.

STUDY QUESTIONS

1. What past event (events) do you need to let God help you let go of?

2. Spend a few moments reflecting on how the members of your family are gifts to you. Now resolve to find ways to tell each member of your family that their love is a precious gift in your life.

3. Where and how do you need to find your voice in speaking the truth to the ordained so that our church can become more functional and healthy?

Chapter XII

STEWARDSHIP: TIME TO START LIVING THE DREAM

It happens to all men and women
the time when scattered pieces come together
to form a whole, and if they are aware,
forever after they can name the hour, the day,
the special nuances of light and shade that shaped the miracle.
Whenever it happens, you will be aware
of seeing visions others do not see
and hearing music others have not heard.
The distant blur will fade and all things
come sharply clear,
henceforth and for all time, you will be different
and you will know the shining difference.

Emma McLaughlin
The Turning Point

We come to the end of our exploratory journey. Some I am sure dropped off along the way. Maybe stewardship was not what they need at this time. Maybe I was not a convincing guide. Maybe they will pick up this book at a later time and they will be in a better place in their lives. I wish that everyone were ready to embrace and be embraced by the spirituality of stewardship because I know how much that spirituality has enriched my life. I am grateful for the time they have spent with us.

I am more grateful for you who are still on the journey with me. What happens now?

Seven frogs were sitting on a log. Four decide to jump off the log. How many are left on the log? Many will answer three but that is not the correct answer. The correct answer is seven. Why? Because there is a big difference between deciding to jump and actually jumping. There is a big difference between knowing about stewardship and making the leap of faith to become a steward of all God's gifts. "Chapter V: The Christian Steward" of the Bishops' pastoral letter *Stewardship: A Disciple's Response* is introduced by this quote from Archbishop Thomas J. Murphy, who was at the time the archbishop of Seattle and is now considered by most to be the father of stewardship for the Catholic Church in America, "It was sixteen years ago, but it seems like only yesterday, I was suddenly confronted with serious surgery, which I never thought would happen to me. It always happens to others. The memory is still there, and I recall vividly the days before the surgery. I really received the grace to ask myself, 'What do I own and what owns me?' When you are wheeled into a surgery room, it really doesn't matter who you are or what you possess. What counts is the confidence in a competent surgical staff and a good and gracious God. I know that my whole understanding and appreciation of the gifts and resources I possess took on new meaning. It is amazing how a divine economy of life and health provides a unique perspective of what really matters." Serious surgery and a deep personal faith helped Archbishop Murphy change his priorities and how he viewed his possessions. Hopefully we can learn from his experience and not have to wait until "our time on earth" seems to be coming to an end before we embrace more fully the spirituality of stewardship.

"What do I own and what owns me?" All of us need to meditate on that profound question over and over again! It is so easy to be overwhelmed by our things. In our time, being owned by our possessions is sometimes cleverly referred to as "affluenza," which is but a new word for an ancient problem. Remember this parable from Luke's gospel, "There was once a rich man who, having had a good harvest from his land, thought to himself, 'What am I to do? I have not enough room to store my crops.' Then he said, 'This is what I will do: I will pull down my barn and build bigger ones, and store all my grain and my goods in them and I will say to my soul: My soul you have plenty of good things laid by for many years to come; take things easy, eat, drink, have a good time.' But God said to him, 'Fool! This very night the demand will be made for your soul; and this hoard of yours, whose will it be then?' So it is when a man stores up treasure for himself in place of making himself rich in the sight of God." (Lk 12:16-21)

Remember one of the foundational pillars of stewardship—**everything we have is a gift from God**. We need to stop turning God's gifts into problems. Gifts become problems when we lose balance in our lives. I remember seeing a bumper sticker once that said, "Jesus is coming. Look busy!" That is certainly a case of turning the precious gift of time into a problem. Luke's Gospel (Lk 10:38-42) gives us the wonderful story of Jesus' visit with Martha and Mary. Martha is worried about the details of the visit; Mary is content to sit at the feet of Jesus and listen to him. The gift of a visit by Jesus quickly became a problem. Why? Because balance was lost. Martha lost balance because she had no time to spend with her guest. Mary lost balance because she neglected the details of hospitality. In the Gospel Jesus tells Martha that Mary "has chosen the better part." Given the choice of hospitality or being present to a guest, Jesus said, "Be present!" However, we know that the choice should not be either/or but both/and. Being present is important; hospitality is important. They need to be in balance, not in opposition. Patricia Datchuck Sanchez, writing commentary for Celebration Preaching Resources, offers some very compelling insights into this section of Luke's Gospel. "To love God, to love Jesus and to welcome the divine presence into our lives requires a decisive and ongoing receptivity to the grace, peace and light that God alone can offer. A life that is too busy, a life whose priorities are askew or whose values are not clearly defined will become dissipated and distracted." In another section of that same resource she offers further insight into the necessity of living a balanced life. "In a society that seems to revel in 60-70 hour work weeks and wears the title 'workaholic' like a badge of honor, today's Gospel presents a challenge of balance, i.e., balancing work with play as well as prayer with service. As Gordon Dahl once observed, 'Many middle-class Americans tend to worship their work, to work at their play and to play at their worship. As a result, their meanings and values are distorted. Their relationships disintegrate faster than they can keep them in repair, and their lives resemble a cast of characters in search of a plot'." The spirituality of stewardship will keep our lives in balance. It will align our priorities and define our values. Rather than being distracted we will be focused. Why? Because everything we have is a gift from God. We will receive God's gifts with gratitude. We will never let God's gifts become problems because we will develop them responsibly and share them lovingly with others. In so doing our lives are both balanced and enriched and we become better people whose lives are pleasing to God.

I hope you remember the quote from Anthony DeMello that closed out Chapter I: "I used to be stone deaf, I would see people stand up and go through all kinds of gyrations. They called it dancing. It looked absurd to me—until one day I heard the music!" I said then that the music of stewardship was planted in our hearts the day we were baptized. The problem is too often we do not hear that music so we fail to dance in the presence of our God. My stated purpose back then was to help you hear the music of stewardship. Hopefully I have had some success and, no matter how tentatively, you have begun to dance with gratitude in your heart for all God's gifts. Do not worry if others see the change in your life; don't worry if they think what you are doing is absurd. Hopefully you can slowly help them hear the music of Stewardship and begin to dance with you.

Several years ago on my winter vacation I was reading what I call "a mindless murder mystery." I do not remember the title or the author but I do remember the quote, "There are too many rowboat people in the world." The author then went on to develop the idea that the problem with rowboat people is that they go forward while looking backwards. There has to be an occasional peek forward but most of the attention is focused on where the rower has been, not where the rower is going. Our faith and our spirituality are a lot like that. We may grow. We may indeed move forward but our focus is on the security of where we were, not where we are going. Once the rowboat people quote was in my head it kept bouncing around disturbing my peace of mind. Finally, I realized that I needed another image and the Holy Spirit came to my rescue. Slowly I began to think about how we need to get out of the rowboat and get into a sailboat. In a sailboat we go forward while looking forward. We need the wind if we are to go anywhere. The wind, the breath of God, needs to fill our sails. The wind is God's gift. We have to let it fill our sails and our hearts with gratitude. The breath of God, the Holy Spirit's gift of inspiration, will sometimes take us where we would not choose to go. Sometimes it will be smooth sailing; sometimes we will have to tack. I don't want to get lost in the rowboat/sailboat analogy so let me conclude by saying in a sailboat it is obvious that the power comes from somewhere other than ourselves. The same is true when it comes to being a steward or disciple of God's gifts. The power in our lives comes from God and the spirituality of stewardship helps us let that power move us forward with our eyes wide open.

The Bible reminds us often "God's ways are not our ways." It takes courage to embrace the spirituality of stewardship because, like much of our faith, it is counterintuitive. We have been conditioned by our culture to take care of ourselves first. We pile up savings for that rainy day. Once we have finished our work and our free time, then and only then will we find time to give to others. We will share our talents if we are not too tired or too busy. Stewardship invites us to share our gifts as an ongoing part of our lives and not from the dregs of our lives. "Then he said to all, 'If anyone wants to be a follower of mine, let him renounce himself, take up his cross every day and follow me. For anyone who wants to save his life will lose it; but anyone who loses his life for my sake, that man will save it. What gain, then, is it for a man to have won the whole world and to have lost or ruined his very self? For if anyone is ashamed of me and my words, of him the Son of Man will be ashamed when he comes in his own glory and in the glory of the Father and the holy angels'." (Lk. 9: 23-26) Gratefully sharing God's gifts, stewardship, is an integral part of living out our Baptism; it is not a nice addition if we feel like it.

Among the lasting joys that Stewardship has brought into my life are the witness talks given by members of the parish. There is a power in the ways they describe what the spirituality of Stewardship has done for them. Allow me to share some of their witness: "I have never been part of a parish community in which my fellow lay people played such an important and visible role in every aspect of parish life. To me this was and still is very inspiring—seeing so many members of the parish bearing witness to their baptismal call and sharing their God-given gifts with one another in the parish and in the community at large." Another lay witness quoted a well told story and added to it: "Many years ago in England, three men were pouring into a trough a mixture of water, sand, lime and other ingredients. A passer-by asked them what they were doing. The first said, 'I am making mortar.' The second said, 'I am laying bricks.' But the third said,

'I am building a cathedral'." They were all doing the same thing, but each looked at it differently. And what a difference that made.

We can see something similar in the way people relate to their parish. Why they give of their Time, Talent, and Treasure. One person says, "All they do is ask for money," a second person replies, 'Well, you know, I have bills to pay." But the third person says, "I am building the Body of Christ." The three are doing the same thing, but what a difference in their attitude! Another lay witness said, "Stewardship is a responsibility for all ages. It is comprised of Time, Talent, and Treasure. It is about 'needing to give' and not 'giving to needs.' It is about giving of our substance and not of our surplus. I have chosen to focus on the Talent aspect of stewardship because I know that individually and collectively we all have talents. And as Catholics we are called to share our talents in some way or form. For some maybe the seeds have been planted and with further nurturing we will see more growth. For others the planted seeds are ready to burst open." A very busy mother gave this witness: "I mentioned that you can grow your Time and Talent here. Even in the over-hectic times we all share, you may find when you decide to contribute a tiny fraction of your time— your perception of how you spend your time will change. When you feel that you couldn't possibly give or do one more thing for one more person (and who hasn't felt like that now and then) the gift you receive in feeling a sense of truly being a part of what goes on in this parish seems to expand what little time we have."

Learning to embrace Stewardship ideally starts in our families, "Growing up as the oldest of five children, I learned early on about the concept of sharing and I truthfully admit that sometimes I did it out of obligation, not out of the goodness of my heart. My parents raised us to count our blessings instead of focusing on whatever we lacked. We weren't wealthy by any means, but we always had more than we needed and knew that there were many people in our own country and around the world that were suffering and needed our help. With this in mind, I can remember sharing a portion of my newly earned babysitting wages with a local charity as well as donating any toys, books or clothing that were no longer being used to places like the Salvation Army." Another lay witness spoke of the rewards of embracing the spirituality of stewardship, "Embracing stewardship as a way of life has been its own reward. Before I became a lector, I never really spent any time reading and reflecting on scripture. Now I do and so my relationship with God is enriched. Before my husband and I began participating in the marriage preparation classes, we went through our marriage without giving much thought to how we could make it even better. Now we have the opportunity to reflect on our marriage on a pretty regular basis and so our marriage is enriched. Before I became a member of the Liturgy Committee, I came to Mass each week knowing just a few members of this community of faith. Now I have the pleasure of knowing and working with some of those people who used to be just faces at Mass, and so my experience of community has been enriched. On top of all that, I know that even in a small way my involvement has enriched our community. For me, that is the most important thing. The spiritual and personal enrichment are the icing on the cake." This last quote is my favorite of all the lay witness talks I have heard over the years. It was the shortest witness talk I ever heard. The speaker came to church with his Catholic wife and then decided to become a Catholic. I'll let him tell his story, "It was 22 years ago. I'm not sure if this means anything or not: it was Easter, my birthday and I was 33 years old. That following morning I got a call from a woman involved with the C.C.D. program. They were having a potluck supper on Saturday and would I help move the tables and chairs to the Catholic Center on Saturday morning. I said I would. I hung up the phone and said to my wife, 'These Catholics don't waste any time, do they?'…In closing I would like to mention one more thing. If I could remember who made that first phone call to me 22 years ago to ask me to share my time and talents, I would like to say, 'Thank you. You helped change my life'." As we have all heard many times over, "You cannot make this stuff up!" It is not a theory but a fact—stewardship will change your life.

Once of the enduring themes of the papacy of St. John Paul II was *Duc in Altum*! Set out into the deep water! "Now he was standing one day by the Lake of Gennesaret, with the crowd pressing round him listening to the word of God, when he caught sight of two boats close to the bank. The fishermen had gone out of them and were washing their nets. He got into one of the boats—it was Simon's—and asked him to put out a little from the shore. Then he sat down and taught the crowds from the boat. When he had finished speaking he said to Simon 'Put out into deep water and pay out your nets for a catch.' 'Master,' Simon replied, 'we worked hard all night long and caught nothing, but if you say so I will pay out the nets.' And when they had done this they netted such a huge number of fish that their nets began to tear, so he signaled to their companions in the other boat to come and help them; when these came, they filled the two boats to sinking point." (Lk 5:1-7) The key to understanding this Gospel passage is Peter's faith in Jesus and his willingness to "set out into the deep water" and his willingness to believe that Jesus would lead him to holiness.

I firmly believe that the spirituality of stewardship is an invitation to "set out into the deep water." To take the risk of believing that if we follow Jesus' command, the spirituality of stewardship will change our lives.

There is a prayer attributed to Sir Francis Drake that I think is the best way to end this book:

Disturb us, Lord,
when we are too pleased with ourselves,
when our dreams have come true because we dreamed too little,
when we arrived safely because we sailed too close to the shore.

Disturb us, Lord.
when with the abundance of things we possess
we have lost our thirst for the water of life;
when having fallen in love with life
we have ceased to dream of eternity
and in our efforts to build a new earth,
we have allowed our vision of the new Heavens to dim.

Stir us, Lord,
to dare more boldly
to venture on wider seas where storms will show Your mastery;
where losing sight of land, we shall find the stars.
We ask you to push back the horizons of our hopes,
and to push us into the future in strength, courage, hope and love.

This we ask in the name of our Captain, who is Jesus Christ, our
Lord.

Amen